# KIKO

## *How to break the Atlantic rowing record after brain surgery*

**Kiko Matthews**

ISBN HB 978-0-9957368-2-5
ISBN 978-0-9957368-3-2

A catalogue record for this book is available from the British Library

Published in Great Britain
in 2018 by
Polperro Heritage Press
Clifton-upon-Teme, Worcestershire WR6 6DH
United Kingdom
www.polperropress.co.uk

Printed by Orphans Press
Leominster HR6 0LD
United Kingdom

# Contents

## Foreword

I've been a huge admirer of Kiko Matthews ever since she announced her intention to row solo across the Atlantic last year. When she finally set off from Gran Canaria in February, along with many others I avidly tracked her progress and read her gripping blogs, all the time holding my breath until she arrived in Barbados having broken the record for the fastest solo female crossing.

Given her medical history, it was an extraordinary achievement just to have completed the voyage, let alone break the record by several days. Kiko is a remarkable inspiration to so many women and this book not only graphically describes her journey across the ocean but also without a doubt demonstrates how, with courage and determination, almost anyone can achieve the seemingly impossible.

*Dame Katherine Grainger DBE*

*This book is dedicated to the doctors and nurses of King's College Hospital and to Angus Collins for getting me across the Atlantic safely and keeping me entertained for 3,000 miles and sorry for having to live and breathe me and Soma for so long.*

# Introduction

Welcome to the most unusual coffee table book ever. Or maybe it's a self-help book, or an adventure book, or a photography book. I'm not sure what it is, but it's in your hands now so it doesn't really matter!

It's an honest account of me, Kiko, and my solo row across the Atlantic. What got me there, my background, my thoughts on those who have helped me and some of the theories behind my mental strength. I really hope you can take something away from it. I want it to make you laugh, to think and inspire you to challenge yourself. If you cry, that wasn't the intention, but you never know! I want it to make you realise you can do anything. After all, I went to quite a lot of effort to prove to you that anything is possible if you want it enough.

When I was ten, I was on BBC Television with John Humphrys along with the rest of my family. We were bought up without a television and our family was the focus of whether TV affects family life. John turned to my Dad and said, "Don't you think you are putting your children at a disadvantage in life, not having a TV?".

Twenty-six years later, I was being interviewed by him again, for the BBC Radio 4 *Today* programme. Ten hours earlier I had broken a world record solo rowing the Atlantic and was on my way to raising over £100k for the hospital that had saved my life from a life-threatening disease! I've also been told it's the only time John wasn't sarcastic, argumentative or rude to the interviewee. I didn't mention the comment he'd made earlier in my life, but it made me smile!

# The Challenge

In February 2018 I set out to row, solo and unsupported, 3,000 miles across the Atlantic.

I was not only looking to add my name to the handful of five women who had successfully made the crossing solo, but also aimed to cross the ocean in a world record time of 45 days – 11 days less than the current record of 56 days. The carbon fibre, world-class boat that I used already held the world record for the fastest solo male crossing.

The plan was to follow in the direction of the trade-winds, aiding my crossing, but that did not mean it would all be plain sailing. The weather was to play a large part in the comfort of the row and I expected to encounter anything from mirror calm to 40ft waves, not to mention, dark nights rowing, flying fish in the face, sleep deprivation, muscle pains, blisters, sea-sickness, loneliness and potential hallucinations

I had never rowed or been to sea before deciding on the challenge in September 2016. Over the years, I have set myself goals that push my mental and physical boundaries. This would be my biggest to date.

I have found the experiences that come with tackling the unknown and the potential for achievement far outweigh the possibility of failure. With a belief that the outcome is irrelevant, challenge is an opportunity to develop skills and knowledge as well as resilience, confidence and relationships.

Setting off at last, watching Gran Canaria slowly disappear from sight. 3,000 miles to go!

# DAY 1

### THURSDAY, 1ST FEBRUARY

I set off from Puerto de Mogán, Gran Canaria, at 9am watched by Mum, Dad, sister Emmie and my god-daughter as well as Angus Collins, a friend and weatherman, and the film crew.

A little over an hour later, about three nautical miles out, I suddenly remember I've forgotten to take my all-important medication out of the fridge in the apartment I stayed in last night. My growth hormone injections are essential for what I'm doing – my muscles won't work properly without it. So I row all the way back to the marina and find them in the dustbin where the cleaning ladies had put them! I was never going to leave in a normal fashion.

After a pint and some fish at the pub, I set off again – on my own. The last week has been so hectic that it's no surprise I forgot my meds. It was strange coming back from a send-off but I quite liked the solo departure! It was pretty cool leaving and seeing Gran Canaria disappearing in the distance and also weird sleeping at sea. Positive vibes, confused seas and big rolling waves. Winds not as strong as expected but loving being at sea. Adrenaline levels high.

Distance travelled today: 27.37 nautical miles

Day 1
Day 5
Day 10
Day 15
Day 20
Day 25
Day 30
Day 35
Day 40
Day 45
Day 50

# GROWING UP

My first ambition was to be a gypsy. My grandfather was a Smith, a solid gypsy name, so maybe it's in the blood. I was born the third of four children. We had no TV and my Dad would keep road kill in the deep freeze along with the peas, fish fingers and reduced frozen groceries. I was named Sakiko. I ran around without clothes for as long as it was appropriate (aged 10!). I was always the one who was dared to do the dangerous stuff and was always trying to keep up, trying to impress, and be accepted by the big boys. I always wanted to be one of them and as a result had some really bad short haircuts and short shorts. Aged three, I would get cross with Mum or Dad, pack my rucksack with teddies and run away down the drive. When no one chased me, I would cry and turn back. I used to get sent to the downstairs toilet at night when I was naughty but this punishment was short lived because I would make it all cozy and turned it into a treat!

I think that was the beginning of my love of small spaces. I loved the outdoors, I loved nature and I loved camping. School (three in total) was a breeze and I got bored and moved. Again and again. I loved learning, the Army cadets, Duke of Edinburgh, learning music, science, sports, chemistry, boys, getting involved, being cheeky and never doing anything to my best. I was never going to be a prefect (or perfect).

After my desire to be a gypsy, I decided a sweet shop owner would be more fun, then a farmer, vet, forensic scientist, doctor, colour chemist, biochemist, and teacher (I did that for a while). Who knows what they want to do ? I'm still searching, still learning.

# DAY 2

## FRIDAY, 2ND FEBRUARY

On the oars at 4.30am and now simply rowing and sleeping. No appetite at the moment and everything I eat is too salty, too sweet, too much. Think it's the seasickness patch I have on. Through the day, waves gathered and the expected storm arrived. By the time it was evening the waves were pretty hectic.

I hatched down for a longer than normal nap so no massive distance today. Realising that autopilots are a bit of a pain as they turn themselves off whenever they feel like it, which means my course changes without notifying me. Annoying if trying to get a relaxed sleep but not the end of the day.

Getting out in the middle of the night, waves crashing everywhere, in my waterproof jacket (thanks Zhik) and little else(!) isn't much fun in the dark but it has to be done - a bit of a sight for sore eyes though, I'm sure. I dread to think. Thank God it's only me!

Distance travelled today: 44.09 nautical miles
Total travelled 71.46 nautical miles.

**Gran Canaria**

Day 1

Day 5

Day 10

Day 15

Day 20

Day 25

Day 30

Day 35

Day 40

Day 45

Day 50

**Barbados**

# DAY 3

## SATURDAY, 3RD FEBRUARY

Up at 4.30am. The wind noises are mad. I keep hearing people talking (clearly not, though). Puked overboard as soon as I ate my cereal. Weird. Waves are ginormous but just swell, nothing more than something to look at in awe. Learning about the boat's capabilities - she is sweet!

I'm pretty sure there were two that were at least 80 feet. I'm not one for exaggerating but they were definitely twice the size of the other 'massive' waves which I assume were the 40 feet ones everyone speaks of. Being carried up on these waves, reaching the top, praying that the top doesn't break on you (but knowing there is little you can do) until you're there, looking out with a view to die for, ironically, and in anticipation of the one to follow. You drop back down into the trough as the wave moves from under you, and the same praying process begins.

Was I worried? Momentarily, until I remember two things: (1) I have no control so worrying is pointless, and (2) what's the worst that can happen?!

Distance travelled today: 55.66 nautical miles
Total travelled 127.12 nautical miles.

**Gran Canaria**

Day 1
Day 5
Day 10
Day 15
Day 20
Day 25
Day 30
Day 35
Day 40
Day 45
Day 50

# MY UNCONVENTIONAL FAMILY

Dad, a retired GP, spent most of my childhood earning the money. I always remember us having a day which was 'Daddy's treat', camping and bird watching for me when I was seven or eight. He is now a walking encyclopaedia and professional potterer in the garden; loves moth catching and identification.

Mum, three weeks Dad's senior (and definitely in charge!) is the quiet, more spiritual one of the family. She wild swims in the freezing cold, writes people beautifully thoughtful cards, thinks and listens and is very diplomatic. She struggles to get a word in among the rest of us but is probably the central pillar of the family.

Robin, brother No.1, is the sensible one in the family, takes after Dad but with strong diplomatic qualities of Mum. Married to Sophie, with a lovely house in Ealing and a proper job needed to support London life with four kids. He owned a Robin Reliant (three-wheeler car for the youngsters out there) and if it wasn't for 'Bean' I would never be able to throw a ball properly.

Emmie, my only sister, is a law unto herself. Very kind and generous, she also holds the record for the single highest investment on Dragons Den and has had more boyfriends and jobs/businesses than I can count. Considering she didn't really want children, she managed to pop out four very funny, lovely and individual kids of whom Suki, No.3, is my god-daughter.

My younger brother Duncan, the do-er, maker and problem solver of all things mechanical, wooden or whatever. Obsessed with cars and making a dodgy quid or two - we always joke he'd charge his family full price for anything! A doting husband to Julia and dad to his #1.

Sandwiched between three siblings and encouraged to be my own person, it was no surprise I ended up how I did...

# DAY 4

### SUNDAY, 4TH FEBRUARY

Didn't row last night as it was insane. I couldn't see diddly squat and a midnight capsize is my nightmare. Fortunately, the wind direction meant I was still travelling forward. Close call on the capsize Today's waves made me realise how massive the ones before were. Rowing at night was manically phosphorescent, big moon and the darkness really heightens everything. Called it a day after I realised my rowing wasn't making a difference to speed so actually got a slightly longer night sleep. All I think about is bed and the safety of my cabin. Luckily I'm not hungry because using my gas cooker is a bit hairy in this weather and I can survive on the snacks I have or just use cold water.

Distance travelled today: 65.59 nautical miles
Total travelled 192.71 nautical miles.

Day 1
Day 5
Day 10
Day 15
Day 20
Day 25
Day 30
Day 35
Day 40
Day 45
Day 50

# OTHER ATLANTIC CROSSINGS

The first time I crossed the Atlantic was 20 years ago when I was sixteen and was one of 12 British cadets to have won a place on a cadet leadership course to the Yukon, Canada in 2005. The course itself included white-water canoeing, rock-climbing and mountaineering as well as a four-day expedition across a glacier. It was pretty tough and I remember the first few days after arriving there seemed pretty horrible, but after a while we all got used to it. The scenery that we saw there was amazing; mountains, trees, canyons, rivers, and plenty of local wildlife including moose, eagles, beavers and even a bear. This trip really gave me a feel for the wilderness and adventure.

Five years on, I headed to California to sell encyclopaedias door-to-door. I'm not sure I was the most studious door-to-door sales person; when I could do all my work in a morning and evening, I didn't see the point of working 13 hours a day. The swimming pool was far better. Needless to say, I lasted two weeks, moved to Sacremento for a week as a cocktail waitress, lived in someone's walk-in wardrobe, bought a car, realised it was a waste of time and so went home. A somewhat less successful Atlantic trip!

**Cadet ready to meet Canada challenge**

## Expedition on glacier

A TESTING time awaits a Herefordshire teenager about to embark for Canada on an arduous challenge course.

Kiko Matthews, of Breinton, is one of only 12 UK young-sters chosen to take part in the Banff Exchange.

Kiko, 16, is a fifth form pupil at Hereford Cathedral

School and member of its Combined Cadet Force (Royal Navy section).

At the Banff national park in Canada she and nearly 200 other cadets will undergo courses on leadership, orien-teering, search and rescue, survival and communications. Evaluation in the field follows over several days and includes white-water canoeing, rock-climbing and mountaineering. The end comes in a four-day expedition across a glacier.

◄ Hereford Cathedral School cadet Kiko Matthews

# DAY 5

### MONDAY, 5TH FEBRUARY

Body still feeling good today. Not blasting it as still have ages to go, plus I want to enjoy my time, no rush - it's about the journey. Have discovered that baby wipes soaked in surgical spirit help massively with my spotty chafed bottom! Total travel as of 10.30am is 215 nautical miles (a few miles off the 45 day target). I'm doing the maths continuously to make sure I'm on track!

I've generally been struggling with food but have now managed two large packets of freeze dried food in 80 hours. Totally loving it but needing sleep all the time! Body taking its time to adapt. Must be a shock. I wonder what's going on in there?

Distance travelled today: 65.32 nautical miles
Total travelled 258.03 nautical miles.

Gran Canaria

Day 1
Day 5
Day 10
Day 15
Day 20
Day 25
Day 30
Day 35
Day 40
Day 45
Day 50

Barbados

# DRIVING HOME

After university, I became involved in 'Driving Home' – an overland trip driving from UK to Cape Town. The expedition was inspired by Colin Javens who had been paralysed from the shoulders down as a result of a diving accident when he was a student. After the accident Colin and his best friend Ben (my fiancée at the time), had talked themselves into what was going to be an epic feat of perseverance and resilience.

Colin drove every mile of the journey in his especially adapted Land Rover. We were a team of six, all with carefully selected roles, but the 14,000-mile journey through some of Africa's hardest terrain, took its toll. Colin, lost 15kg in weight, accidentally sustained third degree burns in addition to other nasty infections and there were times when we doubted the expedition would even make it. On top of that, four months from the end, in Ethiopia I realised that my engagement to Ben wasn't meant to be and so I called it off. There were many times when I just wanted to jump ship but I couldn't leave. We were a team, each with a job we depended on each other for, and I believed in what we were doing.

It was tough but eventually we made it to Cape Town together and it was a success. It really taught me that if you want something enough, it can be achieved. Purpose, belief and charity. We also raised over £500,000 for spinal related charities in UK and Africa and Colin ended up marrying Chrissy, his personal assistant for the trip. Amazing.

# DAY 6

## TUESDAY, 6TH FEBRUARY

Couldn't wake myself up for my 4.30am start but after a brief look at the chart and my speed I realised an extra hour of sleep wasn't going to hurt anyone. One of the benefits of solo rowing is you can do what you like when you like. If you win, it's your glory; if you lose you're the only one to blame. Sleep was more important. Thank God for favourable winds.

Once out in the water I absolutely love it. The massive waves, the colours, the two little storm petrels, the comfort of my cabin and my mega 200 power ballads and 100 classical tunes! I'm feeling a bit guilty in fact. My boat is good. Why am I enjoying this so much? Also wondering if this is the gentle training for what's to come! Totally love the massive rolling swells that stand next to me and my little boat and before I know, I'm on top looking down into this dark pit. They're pretty innocuous though. Also enjoying the freedom  (ironically, I'm totally controlled by all the elements out here so not so free at all in some way). Spotty sore bottom is having a major makeover thanks to some Proshield Vaseline type cream my friend who is in a wheelchair gave me. Lifesaver. No aches or pains which is great but have to consciously make sure I'm not gripping handles as don't want 'claw hand'!

Distance travelled today: 71.02 nautical miles
Total travelled 329.05 nautical miles.

Day 1
Day 5
Day 10
Day 15
Day 20
Day 25
Day 30
Day 35
Day 40
Day 45
Day 50

# EARLY CAREER

My early childhood was spent wanting to be a traveller, then a farmer, vet, criminal pathologist and doctor. I was brought up earning and saving money from a young age and the 'jobs chart' was one of those family things that one can never forget. 3p for emptying the dishwasher, 2p for clearing the table after lunch, and 5p for closing the curtains around the house. Mega bucks! It all added up and at the end of the week, with 20p pocket money, I soon realised the value of money and work. It taught me independence and that hard work pays. My first paid job was licking envelopes for my Dad (disgusting), waitressing at 14, babysitting and the other usual teenage jobs.

After a false start at Edinburgh University, I took a year out, travelled and worked for directory enquiries ('BT Kiko speaking, which name please?'). I reapplied and ended up at Newcastle studying Molecular Biology where I had a bar job from day three, right up to the end. In the middle of my degree I took a year off for no particular reason and ended up de-boning chickens in a factory. I got a First-class honours, moved back home and designed labels for a pharmaceutical company. Weirdly, none of these really screamed out at me as long-term career solutions and as I've never been attracted to making large amounts of money, a city or office job was not on the cards either.

After driving to Cape Town (Driving Home), I returned to do a PGCE in secondary science at Exeter. Teaching meant long holidays and worldwide travel opportunities. I eventually got a job in Wimborne, Dorset, and the excitement of learning to teach was hard work but rewarding. For a while. Something wasn't right, but I couldn't put my finger on it, so I applied for a job in Leatherhead. Closer to London, longer holidays and more outdoor adventure and sport opportunities for the kids and us as teachers. Then, during the summer holidays, something happened that would change me forever...

# DAY 7

## WEDNESDAY, 7TH FEBRUARY

One week down. I've survived this far. Whoop! Am I meant to be enjoying it this much? Slowly and surely I'm eating away at the miles. Don't think there is anything mega to report. Filled up my 8, 10, 12th litre of water. I'm a bit of a camel it seems (that means I've only drunk 12 litres in seven days and I'm feeling fine). Also feeling mega blessed that I'm here able to experience this. I quite often have to remind myself where I am and what I did to get here. Wondering how long the week one high will last before the novelty wears off.

After I wrote this I ended up naked and nearly capsizing. Lost my sense of humour temporarily but then back on the oars (most comfortable position to be in these conditions) and life was good again!

Weather and daytime temperature is pleasant but chilly at night especially if I get wet (frequent, and often involves a short, sharp curse!)

Distance travelled today: 67.70 nautical miles
Total travelled 396.75 nautical miles.

Day 1
Day 5
Day 10
Day 15
Day 20
Day 25
Day 30
Day 35
Day 40
Day 45
Day 50

# CUSHING'S DISEASE

I was diagnosed with a rare life-threatening condition called Cushing's disease in 2009. It is caused by a tumour on the pituitary gland at the base of the brain which results in the body producing too much cortisol hormone.

At the time I was barely strong enough to climb the stairs or get myself out of a bath due to muscle wasting. Diabetes, insomnia, memory loss, psychosis, osteoporosis, spots, excessive hair growth and puffiness in the face and stomach were just some of the symptoms I had. My cortisol levels were nearly off the scale by the time Cushing's disease was diagnosed and I was admitted to King's College Hospital. At one point my potassium levels dropped so low that I was sent to intensive care where I was monitored round the clock for 24 hours. In the right place in case my heart stopped. It was more serious than I realised!

At one point the operation involved the surgeon drilling into my skull via my nose, removing the tumour on my pituitary gland. By the end of the year I was back to work again and getting fit. But when the symptoms returned in 2017 I had to undergo yet another operation at King's.

During this time I realised that worrying was a waste of time. I had no control of the situation, so what was the point? The energy I saved meant I could use what little I had to help keep me alive and my recovery – a mantra I'd take with forever more. Worrying is a waste of energy.

# DAY 8

### THURSDAY, 8TH FEBRUARY

Hectic and nasty night. Tired and low energy so resting. Taken extra meds. Cloudy and batteries low so COG and SOG* maybe off for a few hours. Sunshine please!

Everything is damp and my cabin goes from being damp and cold to hot and sticky. We had a sideways capsize (not full) at night which meant everything heavy went off to the side and I lost my Parmesan (had it outside keeping cool)! These strong winds are relentless. Amazing for speed but you can't lose focus for a minute. Every time you go in or out of the cabin you have to check for a big wave. Definitely the hardest day, but now the honeymoon period is over, and while these winds keep at me, it's probably inevitable. I have to keep reminding myself 'it's only temporary' and why I'm doing this, and the people of King's College Hospital who I hope will benefit. Eating becoming a bit of an issue but no aches or pains so that's a relief. Perhaps I'm not working hard enough!

[*COG = Course over ground (direction); SOG = Speed over ground (knots)]

Distance travelled today: 78.70 nautical miles
Total travelled 475.45 nautical miles.

**Gran Canaria**

— Day 1
— Day 5
— Day 10
— Day 15
— Day 20
— Day 25
— Day 30
— Day 35
— Day 40
— Day 45
— Day 50

**Barbados**

# KING'S COLLEGE HOSPITAL

Having spent a month at King's College Hospital in London and 24 hours in the intensive care unit there, I wanted to give something back for the amazing care I received from everyone there. The days I spent there in 2009 were the most critical, and the most boring of my life. My abiding memory is of seeing my mother's pain-stricken face each day and seeing her fear that I was about to die. I was always confident that the doctors and nurses would and were doing their best and it was all pretty much out of my control. Letting go of the worry and control made the whole experience far easier, especially when I knew I was in the best care in the UK. I am so grateful to the King's staff for pulling me and my family through that awful time, as anyone who has spent time in a hospital or ICU, whether as a patient or as a family member, will attest.

King's College Hospital was fundraising for a new state of the art Critical Care Centre to be built on the top of the hospital, with a garden that allows for the life support machines to be still connected when outside, a view over Ruskin Park, floor-to-ceiling windows providing natural light and many facilities that will benefit the patients, friends and families. It will be the largest in Europe and will do more than save lives: every part of it will be designed to reduce the damaging effects of staying in critical care. This 121-bed unit, the first of its kind offering fresh air, natural light and outdoor garden for patient wellbeing will make an enormous difference to millions of patients and visitors during their hour of need. I am so honoured to be able to donate more than £100,000 towards the Critical Care Unit at King's.

# DAY 9

## FRIDAY, 9TH FEBRUARY

Distance travelled today: 75.84 nautical miles
Total travelled 551.29 nautical miles.

**Gran Canaria**

Day 1

Day 5

Day 10

Day 15

Day 20

Day 25

Day 30

Day 35

Day 40

Day 45

Day 50

**Barbados**

# RUGBY IN AFRICA

Returning to teach after recovering from Cushing's disease was always the plan. A new job and location but it wasn't long before I started having the same feelings I had at the previous school. I felt trapped. I had nearly died, so this was my second chance. I wanted to love my job and at the time I didn't. But the truth was, I had no idea what I wanted or what was on offer. I was passionate about the environment, but I felt the need to add to that.

In 2011, I quit teaching and volunteered for a project called Rugby In Africa - coaching rugby in Africa alongside a health and social educational programme run by the Bhubesi Pride Foundation.

We planned to introduce rugby to 15 African primary schools in ten different countries, using sport as a platform to empower, unite and inspire local communities. I became the educational coordinator for the project along with five other team mates. This was to be their first expedition, a six-month drive across Africa from UK to Cape Town, stopping at schools along the way. We were a team of four rugby coaches, the team leader and myself in charge of education. Seemed like the perfect job.

I disembarked in Uganda. It wasn't as I had expected and having already done one trip to Cape Town that hadn't gone to plan, I decided there was no need to see this one through. I didn't feel respected and I couldn't stand it any longer. I didn't believe in what I was doing, and the team dynamics were poor. It really taught me that purpose is a strong pillar for success. My first trip I fully believed in and had a true purpose, where as this one, for me, didn't. Purpose and belief, that's what I needed.

# DAY 10

## SATURDAY, 10TH FEBRUARY

Hit the wall! Aren't enough hours in a day to sleep and row. Obsessing about data and how long, how far, have I got enough loo rolls (it's a serious matter as I only took three rolls).

Distance travelled today: 87.00 nautical miles
Total travelled 638.29 nautical miles.

**Gran Canaria**

Day 1
Day 5
Day 10
Day 15
Day 20
Day 25
Day 30
Day 35
Day 40
Day 45
Day 50

**Barbados**

# LATER CAREER

I was in Uganda with no real direction when I was offered a teaching job at a local ex-pat school so there I stayed and played (perhaps a bit too hard). Jinja was the source of the Nile and land of the raft guide. I met up with one of those guides in a bar – a good-looking guy who, as it turned out, actually taught stand-up paddle-boarding (SUP). The ulterior motive plan was to book a lesson with him and paddle off together into the sunset. I fell in love with it, not him! When I returned to the UK I decided that I wanted more purpose in my life and a career out of the things I loved and believed in - SUP, the environment, outdoors, adventure and teaching.

With no money to my name and no idea what I wanted to do, I returned to teaching. Soon the same feelings about my career as a teacher returned. I got a part time job as Head of Science and in my spare time investigated how to set up a charity. I met a guy called Charlie Head, a SUP adventurer, who helped change my life forever.

Together we set up The Big Stand charity – based around SUP, it would empower with education and inspire through adventure. It had no resources, I had left teaching and needed an income so I set up SUPKiko, giving paddle-boarding lessons in Richmond and Hackney. I worked with Help for Heroes, helping fundraise for charities and my customers gain confidence. Trash4Treats was one of the main things to be born from SUPKiko and I loved it. Collecting litter from the canal in Hackney, customers would be rewarded from The Milk Float café with a treat. Happy business, clean canals and fulfilled customers. 80-hour weeks were easier than Monday mornings as a teacher and amazing things could be achieved when the main goal was not about making money.

# DAY 11

### SUNDAY, 11TH FEBRUARY

The wall I hit is getting lower. Adaptation time. The past week has been relentless. Relentless is my name for the trip. Relentless rowing, damp, need for sleep, lack of love for food (if you need a forced diet, this is one hell of a way to lose weight)! Winds dropping which is good and bad. Less than 2,000 nautical miles to go. What can I do it in? I'd love to beat my target of 45 days.

Distance travelled today: 76.85 nautical miles
Total travelled 715.14 nautical miles.

— Day 1
— Day 5
— Day 10
— Day 15
— Day 20
— Day 25
— Day 30
— Day 35
— Day 40
— Day 45
— Day 50

# LATER CAREER

*Trash For Treats in Hackney*

# CHALLENGE & COMMUNITY

As a team player (ironically) and having been single for most of my adult life, I have always been drawn to women for community and support and have really discovered the power of working together with other people. Challenging myself has really lead me to be a confident and empowered woman and I am passionate about every other woman (and man) discovering and experiencing what I have.

The campaign itself started as a personal challenge – something to keep me out of mischief but also, having been at a point so close to death, I wanted to show people how life can change and what can be achieved with the right attitude and support. It was also a great opportunity to say thank you to King's College Hospital by raising funds for their new critical care unit to thank them for saving my life. As my journey developed, I reflected a lot and fell in love with the message around the power of challenge in overcoming adversity, developing resilience and becoming empowered as well as the importance of collaboration and community amongst women.

I set up 100TogetHER, avoiding corporate sponsorship, to try and involve one hundred (or more) women in my record attempt and to promote community and collaboration – showing that any challenge can be overcome or achieved if we work together and support one another. With the photos of every woman inside my cabin, the team was incremental in not only getting me to the start line but also emotionally powered me across the Atlantic. Each 'woman' (group, business or individual) was asked to donate £1k in exchange for a package of goodies as well as being part of a community of awesome women and the world record team.

# DAY 12

## MONDAY, 12TH FEBRUARY

Blue skies, not enough wind and I must stop counting down days. The wind will do what it will and I'll arrive when I arrive. I cleaned the bottom of the boat and my hair (first in two weeks)! Sleeping is an issue. At night my body becomes paralysed and physically can't get up. It's tiring and the hours are going slower. Eating is still an issue and probably consuming little more than 1,500 calories a day and even that is a struggle. Hoping that a monster appetite will appear at some point. Probably all related to the medical condition but who knows. I look out at the horizon and wonder a) how the hell did I end up here, b) where is everyone, and c) I'm sure I was here yesterday (and will be here again tomorrow). Found two dead flying fish onboard. Poor little things! Didn't eat them.

Distance travelled today: 63.05 nautical miles
Total travelled 778.19 nautical miles.

Gran Canaria
Day 1
Day 5
Day 10
Day 15
Day 20
Day 25
Day 30
Day 35
Day 40
Day 45
Day 50
Barbados

# THE SOLO RECORD

The fastest woman to row solo across the Atlantic before me was Anne Quéméré from France who completed the crossing in 2003 in 56 days, 13 hours and nine minutes. She started from La Gomera in the Canaries and arrived in Guadeloupe in the West Indies. More recently, Elaine Hopley became the fastest woman in an open-class boat to complete the east-west crossing in 59 days in 2017.

I made the crossing in the same open-class boat, *Soma*, that held the solo male record before the awesome Dutchman Mark Slats achieved the current overall solo record of 30 days, seven hours and 49 minutes. I can't imagine that ever being broken.

My aim was 45 days - an arbitrary number halfway between 35 and 56 but the chances of that were slim - it's so weather dependent. 49 days, I hope, is a time that someone will be able to beat, or at least have a good go at.

# DAY 13

## TUESDAY, 13TH FEBRUARY

According to my calendar it's day 14 so not sure what happened with the days and dates - so confused! Saw a whale this morning - 10 metres from boat. The wind has gone. Every stroke makes a difference and getting the boat moving makes much more of an effort. I'm starting to feel my arse on my seat and so trying lots of different soft seat options. Living is easier but rowing harder. Still trying to eat more. They say you can lose up to 20% of your body weight doing this which I now totally believe. Dreaming of food. Also stopped the data calculations. I cannot control when I arrive, this wind is its own, so just focusing on being. Love singing out at the top of my voice (usually only one line) and look around to check no one is listening! Stars shining (saw something weird in the sky last night).

Thanks for all your support! Can't believe seven months ago I had just had brain surgery and now I'm here. King's (hospital), I love you!

"Hello from the middle of the Atlantic. Lying here semi-naked having an interesting mental and physical time. Thank you so much for all your support.

Day 1

Day 5

Day 10

Day 15

Day 20

Day 25

Day 30

Day 35

Day 40

Day 45

Day 50

Barbados

Saw a whale this morning, saw some dolphins the other day. It's pretty much like the same thing day in and day out. Row, sleeping, eating, more sleeping, more rowing – getting there, trying not to count down the days but it's hard.

Hoping that I don't run out of loo rolls. I forgot to bring myself enough loo rolls so I've got to get to Barbados quick."

Distance travelled today: 62.13 nautical miles
Total travelled 840.32.14 nautical miles.

# DAY 14

## WEDNESDAY, 14TH FEBRUARY

Once again Mr Postman couldn't deliver my streams of Valentine's cards but instead I spent the day (yet another) looking at where I'd come from, waves, sky and my little storm petrel who visits me daily. It's getting monotonous. The winds are low and every stroke requires energy. My watch is becoming my friend (at the end of the shift) and my enemy (in the middle and during my rest). I'm not even sure I've written this day already!

Distance travelled today: 52.76 nautical miles
Total travelled 893.08 nautical miles.

**Gran Canaria**

Day 1
Day 5
Day 10
Day 15
Day 20
Day 25
Day 30
Day 35
Day 40
Day 45
Day 50

**Barbados**

# THE TUMOUR RETURNS

A year before I set out, I was feeling good. Strong. In fact, on April 23rd (my birthday) I took my rowing machine down to Limehouse, London, and set up a station where I was going to row a marathon (42km), on London Marathon day. I hate the rowing machine as much as I hate the gym. It's indoors and dull. Unfortunately, joining a rowing club was going to cost me money and my life was so variable, I'd probably end up only visiting every so often. As a result, most of my rowing had been out in Soma, my ocean rowing boat. Anyway, I turned up on the Sunday, set up camp and grabbed a tiramisu (which I didn't realise was alcoholic until someone pointed out that it probably wasn't the best pre-marathon fuel!). They were wrong.

The campaign work, meetings, talks, nannying (my pay-the-rent job) was using up most of my energy so training had been put on the back burner a little, plus I was tired. I sat for three hours 17 minutes on the rowing machine, had a meeting whilst rowing, chatted, smiled, and pulled (not a guy, just the cable). I came eighth in the world for 2017 for all women. Well that was easy. I did a similar thing six weeks later but took eight minutes off that time. I was strong and didn't feel like I was really training that hard.

A few weeks later, I was on my mountain bike (kindly donated by an Instagram follower when my previous one got nicked) in London in my 'active wear' and trainers (not the Lycra type) and I'm overtaking pretty much everyone. One guy (I hear they're called MAMILS – middle aged men in Lycra) clearly doesn't like this. His ego is dented and his facial expression looks like his ego feels! I begin to think that overtaking men on bikes is fun, but not normal...

# THE TUMOUR RETURNS

## 2018 42,195m (Marathon) Indoor Rower Rankings

Weight: All | Gender: F | Ages: All | Count
| Verified Results | Adaptive: No

| Pos. | Name | Country | Time |
|------|------|---------|------|
| 1 | Morgan Stewart | USA | 3:06:52 |
| 2 | Kiko Matthews | GBR | 3:09:17. |
| 3 | Lee Alison Crawford | USA | 3:14:22. |
| 4 | Liz | AUS | 3:17:01.8 |

Super strength was something I'd experienced last time I was ill so this was potentially something to be safer than sorry about. My neck and double chins were reasonably evident, and I'd been getting up early without it being an issue. Life was also feeling pretty awesome, my photography was becoming more and more creative, and generally, I was full of energy.

Six weeks later, I'm back at the doctors discussing the MRI results. The tumour has come back and the best course of action was surgery. I'm fit, I've been here before and I've caught it pretty early so all should be fine.

# THE TUMOUR RETURNS

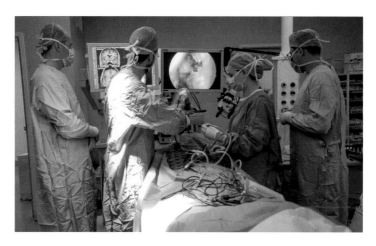

August 1st, I wake up at 5.30am, cycle eleven miles to King's College Hospital and head straight for the pre-op ward. By 6pm I'm awake and tumour free, chatting away with my friends. Three days later I'm out of hospital and ten days after that I'm on my bike doing a 100km bike ride. What doesn't kill you, only makes you stronger (and wiser!).

So there we have it, my tumour, my humour and strength removed, goddammit! Obviously, training had to be a little more chilled due to the fact they had drilled a hole into my brain, but additionally, my cortisol levels had gone from being three times what they should be to four times less than they should. It's like a heroin addict doing cold turkey. Whilst there are drugs, it's still difficult to get them right. Consequently, the following weeks were difficult on the training front.

# DAY 15

## THURSDAY, 15TH FEBRUARY

I'm feeling some niggles in the left side of my body, probably because I spend the majority of my time looking left and using my left oar first, since the waves always approach from the left. On my night shift, I suddenly realise there are some big things down there, glowing. I can't figure if they are patches of individual plankton or something much bigger. I'm still struggling with energy and night. There is no moon; it rises on the horizon in the day, and whether it's my medical condition or me being lazy, I can't make it to row at night. Means I have to make up for it in the day. Feel guilty for long sleeps at night and have to remind myself not to give myself a hard time. Apparently the winds are picking up tomorrow which will be a welcome relief.

I think I have made it one third of the way. This last week has dragged so much. By the end of the day my thumb is numb, my left bum cheek hurts and I can feel the muscle niggle in my left back and a twinge in my left wrist. Must be careful.

Distance travelled today: 42.25 nautical miles
Total travelled 935.33 nautical miles.

**Gran Canaria**

Day 1
Day 5
Day 10
Day 15
Day 20
Day 25
Day 30
Day 35
Day 40
Day 45
Day 50

**Barbados**

# PHYSICAL TRAINING

Guin Batten, a British Olympic rowing silver medallist, wrote me a training programme which I stuck at for a couple of months. I completed the two hours on, two hours off, two hours back on and then the ergo got pushed to one side of my life and my room! For me, exercise needs purpose. Cycling to meetings and to meet friends, SUPing to make money and running up every flight of stairs makes sense. I lived in my 'activewear'! I rowed a few marathons on the rowing machine and joined Roehampton Uni rowing club. After my operation, Fit8 in Wimbledon joined the support team and I started at the gym. My muscles weren't developing as I thought they should and it turned out I was also growth hormone deficient along with the known cortisol deficiency. Injections started and it all reverted to normal.

I'd drive two and a half hours out to Burnham-on-Crouch in Essex (the HQ of ocean rowing), meet up with the crew at Rannoch Adventure and then head out, either up or down the River Crouch. I loved it; it was new, it was always sunny and the photographs of sunrises and sunsets made for some great social media posts. At first, I was nervous anchoring and sleeping in the river, but when I mastered that, I was nervous going out of the mouth. When I mastered that, I was nervous rowing at night, and when I mastered that I was nervous heading up the coast and so on. I knew that if I applied the same mentality and experience outcome to my Atlantic crossing, things would be fine. Big waves were the thing I was most nervous about. I wouldn't say I mastered them, but I survived.

# DAY 16

## FRIDAY, 16TH FEBRUARY

Woke up to what I can only think is Sahara dust. The whole horizon orange and misty. The sun must have been a good hour into the day before it was visible. Winds improved slightly, and I dreamt of pudding and eating fresh broad beans straight off the plant. Oh, and cheese. Lots of cheese but not the Parmesan, that is out there somewhere. My appetite is better but still not eating fully what I'm burning. I saw a ship yesterday, a big one, speeding pretty fast past me. Lucky she wasn't a few miles further north or it could have been interesting! First sign of human life.

I'm stuck with useless weather but learning that I just have to lump it! Another day more! Shame but no probs, things will change (or will they?).

Distance travelled today: 57.58 nautical miles
Total travelled 992.91 nautical miles.

Gran Canaria

Day 1
Day 5
Day 10
Day 15
Day 20
Day 25
Day 30
Day 35
Day 40
Day 45
Day 50

Barbados

# PHYSICAL TRAINING

# TO THE BITTER END

Training on the River Crouch in Essex was a very different experience to being out in the middle of the Atlantic. For one thing, there was a rescue service nearby (a very good one too. RNLI, we love you). The point of training isn't for everything to go to plan, but to learn from mistakes.

During one training session off the Essex coast I made the mistake of throwing my expensive Fortress marine anchor overboard when it wasn't tied on. I had been rowing for eight hours and needed to get back into Felixstowe. With a tail wind and the tide pushing me up the coast, I knew I would not get back in time if I didn't stop. But I misjudged the power of the tide and wind and hadn't tied on the anchor before throwing it over and I literally held on to the bitter end of the rope until I could hold no longer. My anchor was gone. That's where the phrase 'She held on until the bitter end' comes from….

Now, you can't be a solo rower without a sea anchor. You can't stop and rest or sleep and with the tide going out it meant that any of the marinas nearby weren't an option to get into. I had a few words with myself – why did I do that when I know better? What are your options? What are you capable of and what's the weather doing? Worrying was (and still is) a waste of energy. I needed all the energy I could get and it wouldn't change anything.

I rowed for four hours back towards Felixstowe, but my boat was carried with the tide and wind in the opposite direction. It was soul destroying. The sun went down, and four and a half hours after my silly mistake, my boat was finally moving at zero knots! I have never been so excited to see a speed of zero knots.

# TO THE BITTER END

It had been moving, remember, at a speed in the opposite direction to where I wanted to go, despite rowing forwards. Zero knots meant the tide was changing which meant I had seven hours to row into the wind, but with the tide and in the dark, back to where I needed to be. I made it with 15 minutes to spare, legs wobbling, (dehydrated I'm sure), hungry and with a sore bottom.

I reflected on it afterwards and was very pleased to have had the experience. 'What doesn't kill you, only makes you stronger'. I knew that I was capable of staying calm under pressure, and capable of rowing for 19 hours in a 24-hour period. All good things to take with me on my crossing, including a much lighter sea anchor across the Atlantic. Oh, and make sure you tie everything on to the boat before it goes overboard. I won't forget that.

# MAYDAY MAYDAY

I headed out on a two-day row, out of the mouth of the River Crouch towards a wind farm overnight and anchored up as normal beyond the sand banks and round towards the shelter of land. It's a complicated bit of navigation because, at low tide, even my little rowing boat can get grounded (and yes, it did happen once!).

After a reasonable night's sleep at the mouth of the Blackwater, I woke up and realised the weather wasn't really in my favour for getting home. The tide would help a bit, but a southerly wind meant I was going to struggle to get back to the mouth of the Crouch. I suggested heading for the local marina and calling it a day but was advised I could cut off the sandbanks and could get through a little gap. There were strong winds coming which I knew I couldn't row against but when someone more experienced is telling you otherwise, you trust them and go with that.

But my boat started going slower and slower until I was barely moving. The winds were getting stronger and the waves bigger. I anchored and called for advice. The next thing I knew, I was doing a call out to be rescued. I was anchored and safe and no harm would have come to me if I'd waited 24 hours but fortunately the RNLI was close at hand and a rescue ensued. Not ideal, I know, as it was their Sunday afternoon that I had interrupted, and it probably could have been avoided. I hit my head due to the waves and towing (RNLI don't have to tow boats, so this was very kind of them) and all in all I was frustrated that I hadn't stood my ground. It gave me practice of my VHF skills and confidence in my own knowledge and understanding of tides, wind and my ability. Fingers crossed, this wouldn't happen at sea…

# DAY 17

## SATURDAY, 17TH FEBRUARY

The words relentless, temporary, miles, days and Barbados continuously come into my thoughts. I'm sure I was here yesterday. Looks the same. For all I know it could be the same. I wonder if any boat has passed this exact point before or if I'm a first. I forget what I've told you.

My thoughts on the peanuts. Do fish have peanut allergies? I hope not. I've fed them lots of stale peanuts! At what point do they not sink anymore? Where is their density equal to that of the sea water. I imagine different layers of nuts - almonds just above the peanuts, just below the cashews with the chilli puffs floating on top. I watch the occasional comical Disneyesque-looking Portuguese man-of-war and say hello to my daily visit from the storm petrel. I move from side to side changing my bum cheek to get a more comfortable position. I check my watch. Five minutes! I try to do some maths in my head. Days, speeds, how long?

I stop and remind myself it won't make things happen any quicker. I can't believe I've been here 17 days and I have potentially another four weeks. But I am over a third of the way! An achievement but still a long way to go.

Gran Canaria

Day 1
Day 5
Day 10
Day 15
Day 20
Day 25
Day 30
Day 35
Day 40
Day 45
Day 50

Barbados

51

I open a card. It has a picture of a boat with my name on it. OMG, one of my old schools (also part of my 100TogetHER) have named their new fours rowing boat after me. That makes me emotional and very happy. I have a boat named after me! Thank you to everyone at Hereford Cathedral School - an honour.

Distance travelled today: 62.67 nautical miles
Total travelled 1,055.58 nautical miles.

# DAY 18

## SUNDAY, 18TH FEBRUARY

I try to move my body. It has nothing in it. I take my meds and fall back to sleep for an hour. BBC *Breakfast* call me: I try to be normal but it's surreal talking from the middle of the Atlantic to a load of people sitting at home on their sofas on a Sunday morning. Feeling better I get up and go outside. I've done some maths, I wonder if I can do it in 25 more days. Is that realistic? The wind has changed. It's faster and now the boat moves. For the last week, every time I stop for a drink or some food, I then have to get the boat moving in a rhythm again. Today I can't stop it. Every stroke is a delight, the boat dances with the waves and wind. She's happy, I'm happy. Just over 300 nautical miles to the halfway point. Amazing but then I think 'half way'! I've got to do this all again, without the joys of the honeymoon period at the beginning. The moods change so quickly, depending on how you think of a situation or what pops into your head. What message of support or text I get from home. Fragile! But today is a day for rowing. The aches disappear, miles are achieved, good thoughts are had. It's relentless but temporary. I dream of cold fresh vegetables. Anything fresh. And a bed that doesn't throw me from side to side every half minute!

Distance travelled today: 65.54 nautical miles
Total travelled 1,121.12 nautical miles.

Gran Canaria

Day 1

Day 5

Day 10

Day 15

Day 20

Day 25

Day 30

Day 35

Day 40

Day 45

Day 50

Barbados

# MY BOAT

My boat, *Soma of Essex*, was the most advanced and innovative ocean rowing boat ever built, a Rannoch Solo constructed out of lightweight carbon fibre shell and Nomex inner core, making her the strongest, lightest ocean rowing boat for her size. She's self-righting, seven metres in length, five feet wide and her hull is just 10mm thick. In fact, it turned out she was pretty difficult to capsize in the first place.

*Soma*'s design uses Formula 1 technology and aerospace. She's five years old and the Nomex material which she is built with looks like a honeycomb and is made by British Aerospace. The whole structure only weighed 78 kilos when built. It needs to be light for speed as I was rowing half a ton through the water when at sea in her.

It has crossed the Atlantic a few times, but I'm the first woman to use her. She's definitely the best ocean rowing boat in the world, built by Rannoch Adventure and is the same boat that Charlie Pitcher used in 2013 to become the world's fastest solo transatlantic rower with a time of 35 days and 33 minutes.

# DAY 19

## MONDAY, 19TH FEBRUARY

Today was tough. I'm exhausted. Not sure if my medical condition is adding to this, but... dinner time and I inhale a meal! In one sitting. Unheard of. I'm starving. The body is adapting?

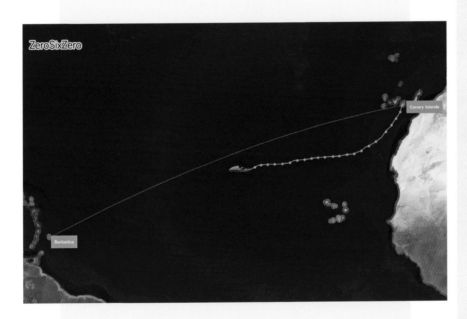

Distance travelled today: 55.69 nautical miles
Total travelled 1,176.81 nautical miles.

Day 1
Day 5
Day 10
Day 15
Day 20
Day 25
Day 30
Day 35
Day 40
Day 45
Day 50

Barbados

# DAY 20

TUESDAY, 20TH FEBRUARY

Has it really been two days since I last wrote? This is bad, I thought it was just a day ago. Says it all really. The days have been much the same recently. I've been playing eye spy with myself. I get enjoyment from small things: my small sweetie bag of jelly worms normally rewarded late afternoon; realising a pain I had has gone, moving my bum cheek a millimetre to the left or right and suddenly it being a whole new experience when my boat, body and wave get in a rhythm. I'm not sure what causes this but it's awesome when it does because it feels so good and the boat moves faster.

Getting an email or text from UK or from people with words of support, especially when it has something about them in it. 'Keep going you're doing a great job' is lovely but it's so great when people personalise my experience and what I'm doing to them.

Sunrise and sunset and the sun's reflection on the water. Sleep. Next blog I'll tell you the simple things that irritate me or put me in a less than positive mood.

Distance travelled today: 54.31 nautical miles
Total travelled 1,231.12 nautical miles.

**Gran Canaria**

Day 1
Day 5
Day 10
Day 15
Day 20
Day 25
Day 30
Day 35
Day 40
Day 45
Day 50

**Barbados**

# PREPARATION

With next to zero idea or experience of running a campaign the size of mine, it was never going to be easy. I wanted to raise £100,000 for King's College Hospital and was also looking for £100,000 for the project itself (although this wasn't what was needed to actually get me and the boat in the water and return both safely home; it was the amount needed to make it successful). It was hard work, plus I had training, some difficult characters to work with very close to the project, my paddleboarding day job and nannying, as well as the little tumour recurrence and surgery. People generally don't like parting with their money but I was amazed by those I met that did and the opportunities that presented themselves. The generosity, the characters, the excuses, the support, the enthusiasm, the disbelievers: I saw everything and met all sorts. It was this part that was the real challenge, although I was often told, if you can get the boat in the water, you're 90% of the way there.

By the end of two years I hope to have raised £150,000 for the Critical Care Unit at King's, and around £50,000 for the project (plus a lot of sponsored kit and services). That's a lot of money raised by many very generous people plus their skills, time and financial support and I'm very proud to say I know most of those people. I'm actually more proud of the success of this part of the challenge than the actual world record itself.

# DAY 21

### WEDNESDAY, 21ST FEBRUARY

Today, 21 days in, I hope to have eaten not only my breakfast but also my two main meals. This is a major breakthrough but I'm still not up to my 6,000 calories. Doubt I ever will to be honest. Still struggling with my sleep. Trying one hour on, 20 minutes off in which time I manage to fully get to sleep. Some mornings I can't even make my body move to get my medication which ironically will wake me up and give me energy. I'm going to try a new system where I set my alarm to take meds before it gets to this point (and caffeine tablet), go back to sleep and then re wake up. Will see.

Cleaned the bottom of the boat again. Actually enjoyed it more this time. No sharks, just 5,000 metres of nothing below me. The little creatures (not sure technically what they are) can slow you down a lot so it's really impotant to do. This time I used my Boots Advantage card to get them off, a top tip from Angus, the weatherman and world record ocean rower. It's amazing how quickly they grow. I wonder how cargo ships do this? My boat is only 21 feet long, not 1,000!

Distance travelled today: 59.86 nautical miles
Total travelled 1,290.98 nautical miles.

**Gran Canaria**

Day 1
Day 5
Day 10
Day 15
Day 20
Day 25
Day 30
Day 35
Day 40
Day 45
Day 50

**Barbados**

# MY VALUES

**Be honest** (my best and worst quality). Some people can't deal with it and I'm sorry for that, but if they can and they can accept me for that, then this is who I want to live and work with. Being honest is the lowest energy state you can live in so learn to love and accept who you are.

**Be kind and thoughtful.** You should always have time for others. And I'm not saying I'm kind 100% of the time, but I try. Smiling. That helps, too. You never know what difference your smile might make and it's free.

**Be free.** Is that a value? Apparently so. Let it go. Got to be free to live. I guess this goes with not worrying. If only everything else was free.

**Respect life.** Its short so make the most of it. Respect other people's views, way of living and needs. You don't know their background. Respect the environment, it's our supermarket, our shelter, our thermostat and playground. Piss it off and it will retaliate.

**Take risks.** They help you learn, grow and be free. Don't be silly. Calculate the risk first. I always ask 'What's the worst that can happen?'

**Have adventures.** A combination of risk taking and being free.

**Be open-minded**. When I was ill, I looked funny and I said funny things. People probably judged me, but they didn't know the back story. More often we don't know the back story. Don't speculate. Don't judge yourself or others.

# MY VALUES

**Material happiness.** Greed is waste. Buying clothes to follow fashion? To be happy, focus on the inside and not the outside. I always think of my time in Africa. So many happy faces, so little stuff.

When I think about it, if I stick to the values, the happier I become. You need to fill your life with things that interest you and make you smile. If you like doing something, do it more, if you find yourself talking about one thing more than others (not Tinder or your boss) then it may be a passion! If it doesn't make you money, go with it and stop trying to build the bank account. Trust me, you can't buy happiness. I'm honest!

# DAY 22

The wind changed today. It's turned to a northerly, pushing me south. Not ideal but not the end of the world. It's amazing how the rollercoaster of the weather and waves really reflect the emotions and my energy. I imagine it's pretty normal but do wonder if the fact that my body doesn't produce cortisol, the hormone that deals with stress, may be contributing to my insane need for sleep and the feeling that the boat weighs a ton at times.

Cortisol is one of the four essential-to-life hormones. Five days without it and you're on your death bed. Low levels cause nausea, depression, low energy, tiredness and muscle fatigue. Perfect! Fortunately, I have meds to regulate this, and normally it's pretty easy - a few weeks of getting to know what my body needs, and I am able to lead a pretty normal life. But there's nothing like doing one of the most stressful physical and mental activities on earth, with a severe deficiency, to make things a little harder. A normal person would increase cortisol production as a result of stress, lack of sleep, excessive physical exercise, irregular eating patterns and new routines. Given this, it's no surprise I'm struggling with my energy. Taking more tablets would be a solution but get it wrong and the high cortisol levels cause muscle breakdown – not ideal.

**Gran Canaria**

Day 1
Day 5
Day 10
Day 15
Day 20
Day 25
Day 30
Day 35
Day 40
Day 45
Day 50

**Barbados**

Hormones are intricate and fascinating chemicals that play a key part in helping us function properly. But the question I ask myself every day out here is whether I'm feeling like this because of my condition or am I making excuses and being lazy. Guess I'll never know; there's no test and no one (apparently) has ever done anything this extreme with secondary Addison's disease so there's no medical research on the case. But I'm pretty sure I'm trying my best, though even that I wonder some days. Am I being harsh on myself or is this all in the mind? I feel guilty when I'm not rowing that I should be able to do more, and I miss having a benchmark of whether I'm doing okay. It's a bit like doing an exam and never getting the results. Anyway, there's a little biology lesson and what my body is going through, as well as the games that the mind plays.

Distance travelled today: 62.09 nautical miles
Total travelled 1,353.07 nautical miles.

# DAY 23

## FRIDAY, 23RD FEBRUARY

There was me thinking I could make halfway in three weeks. Goddam the weather, it's probably more likely to be four weeks. Some pesky little westerly winds have decided to descend upon me - from an insanely hectic speedy start to now going backwards. Slowly, but backwards. I'm lying here on para-anchor, a big parachute that stops me going in the wrong direction and looks like a very funky jellyfish once deployed. Annoying for any speed records but means I have nothing else to do but rest. Rowing at one mile an hour into the wind isn't worth the energy output.

So much about this is accepting you can't control the situation. Not only applicable to being out here but even more so in real life. There is no point me thinking about times and distances when the weather is what it is. Same for you, wherever you may be doing what you're doing. If it's out of your control, you gotta breathe and let go. Save your sanity, it's not worth it.

Body is beginning to feel better. Not sure it's looking better through! My arse is disappearing and spotty, my hands crispy and dry, my boobs seem to be my primary source of calories for my body and are beginning to look like I've breastfed a family. I think I'm developing a pot belly and the body hair

Day 1
Day 5
Day 10
Day 15
Day 20
Day 25
Day 30
Day 35
Day 40
Day 45
Day 50

is beginning to show. Where's the six pack and sexy adventure look that men get when they do this? Prince Charming will not be having any of this when he sees me (unless of course he can see beyond the temporary imperfections!).

Loo roll update. I left with three, have one and a quarter rolls left and I'm not halfway. No need to be a maths genius to figure out the outcome here. On top of this, I decided going on the pill would be best for a trip like this. No one wants a period in hot sweaty, endurance, small boat environments, right? Well, lucky me, this particular pill decided otherwise. How about we give you some half type period for the whole thing, everyday? Not ideal since I was not prepared for this, one bit. So, all in all, loo paper issue never really stood a chance. Dealing with it though.

Off to check on the big jelly fish (para-anchor) and let it out some more. I think this weather should hopefully change soon. By the way, anyone welcome to come say hi in Barbados, or, if you have friends there, please let them know I'm coming. I would love to see some people there. And thanks for all your messages of support; I am getting them, just no time to reply individually.

Distance travelled today: 44.85 nautical miles
Total travelled 1,397.92 nautical miles.

# DAY 24

SATURDAY, 24TH FEBRUARY

"Kiko is on para anchor and we expect her to be on this for 12 hours. The winds are coming from the west, driving her east (the wrong way). By midnight tonight we expect the winds to come from the north, which means she can dive south, which is just what we need because she has a big system above her that could mean another para anchor session."

*Angus Collins*

Distance travelled today: 11.03 nautical miles
Total travelled 1,408.95 nautical miles.

**Gran Canaria**

Day 1
Day 5
Day 10
Day 15
Day 20
Day 25
Day 30
Day 35
Day 40
Day 45
Day 50

**Barbados**

# MY PERSONAL WEATHERMAN

In September 2014, I met Angus Collins and Charlie Pitcher (his uncle) at a fundraising event in London, an evening that went on to change my life forever. Charlie had the world record for the fastest solo male (in the boat I used) and Angus had just got back from becoming the youngest team of four to cross the Indian ocean. He later went on to get two more world records for crossing the Atlantic.

We all became friends and it was normal for me to hear stories of, and watch, other teams cross the Atlantic. I was very familiar with the boats and the training involved and Angus (*right*) never made a big deal of the scale of the challenge. Seeing all the other people doing the crossing and inspired by photos and stories it seemed a perfectly obvious step to have a go myself. Why not, if they could?

When in a boat alone at sea, there has to be someone to help you with weather and navigation and I chose Angus to be that one. Ocean rowing, and the boats associated with it (Rannoch Adventure) is clearly a passion of his, and that's what you need when out there with zero experience and alone. I trusted him to make good decisions and he is certainly someone you'd want in your team.

Every day he'd have to follow my progress and send me updates and ended up being the person I'd phone up (for whatever reason). One of the disadvantages of being a friend and a client! I'm not sure he's the one I'd have chosen to ball my eyes out on but thankfully it didn't really happen. Thanks to him, I got across safely and in one piece – legend! (well, maybe once he got some tears. Sorry Angus!).

# DAY 25

## SUNDAY, 25TH FEBRUARY

I made the halfway point! Nothing to write home about, no flag and no celebration (well, ten minutes extra sleep!). I haven't missed my ciders and weirdly, coffee neither. It's such a simple life that I find it really blissful.

There's absolutely nothing to worry about. Life is dictated by the weather and how I feel (sleep!) and that's it. Today (Sunday) also bought some awesome winds. Fast and in the right direction. A welcome relief from the day before (which I secretly enjoyed having a day at home, so to speak). It's difficult not to get a little 'frustrated' that every mile isn't direct to Barbados at the moment, due to the need to head south away from the big band of westerlies above and towards easterlies below but, like I said, the wind is the wind, and every mile is now a countdown to home. It's a weird mindset change as every mile is always closer but it seems different. I'm actually blissfully happy. It's boring and monotonous and I'm gagging for fresh food but there's no complaints. I'm at one with it all, even the niggles and crap music I have and the ropes and headphones that get tangled and the fact I've had my period (totally unprepared) every day since day 2!

Distance travelled today: 60.16 nautical miles
Total travelled 1,469.11 nautical miles.

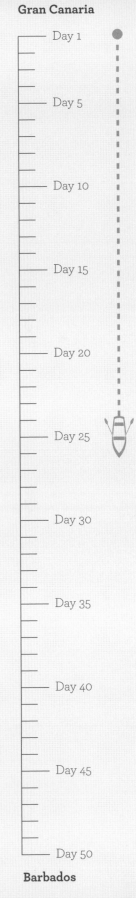

Gran Canaria

Day 1
Day 5
Day 10
Day 15
Day 20
Day 25
Day 30
Day 35
Day 40
Day 45
Day 50

Barbados

# PASSIONS

**The environment** – Where to start? Our planet, the interactions, the balance, life, air, water, the whole lot is amazing. Mind-boggling. It's difficult not to preach and to show people what impact we are having. I get upset that we are so short-sighted and selfish. The only way around this, for me, is to focus on what I can do and maybe other people will follow. I hope it's not too late.

**Travel and adventures** – The more I realised I liked meeting new people, experiencing new cultures and not knowing what was around the corner, the more I realised I couldn't live without these. I ended up in Uganda for a while which has changed my life. I think I've done 41 countries so far.

**Standup paddle-boarding** – I fancied a guy in a bar in Uganda who had some paddleboards and ended up loving it (not him) and went on to set up a charity (The Big Stand) and business (SUPKiko) all based around the sport. It's an amazing combination of physical exercise and mental calm.

**My job** – When people achieve something they didn't think they could do, it makes them happy and that makes me happy. That makes it worth calling it a passion. Interacting with people. It's challenging and ever changing.

**Charity** - I enjoy seeing people benefit from what little I have to offer. It's a weird thing to have  as a passion but if money was no object I'd do free SUP lessons for all and volunteer all day. Pity life costs money.

Can you have that many passions? Mine have given me purpose, enjoyment and happiness. A reason to live. With no sprogs in tow I have to have some purpose to being on this planet, 'cause there ain't no genes being passed on at the moment! There isn't a rulebook of how to find your passion but trying everything helps. I think you need values and to fill your life with things that interest you and make you smile. Follow your passions and stick to your values. Who knows where they will take you ... perhaps even attempting something like what I've just done - rowing solo across the Atlantic Ocean.

# DAY 26

## MONDAY, 26TH FEBRUARY

Bye bye winds, hello north/north westerlies. If you're tracking me, you are probably thinking I'm just chillin' – I'm not, I promise! Today was hot, it's generally getting hotter but with little wind it was time for covering up and dousing myself in water every 30 minutes. Massive shoal of fish came to say hi and I thought there was a hammerhead shark but it turns out to be just wishful thinking. Shame Dad never bought me that fishing kit I asked him to get. Never mind. There is really very little wildlife and I wonder how much I miss because I'm in my cabin or looking the wrong way. Lots of this weird surface seaweed and I love my swooping seagulls that do fly-bys, tilting their wings to just miss the top of the water, watching them using the wind to their advantage. Makes me think of *Top Gun*!

My storm petrel is still around although it clearly gets confused when I change course or go on para-anchor. I wonder where it goes after its five minute check-in, and how far away and how it finds me again. Do they have a built in (Kiko) tracker? Mum thinks it's my Grandma, who died last summer, keeping an eye on me!

Had a very interesting white bird, bit like a parakeet, with a long skinny tail that did some weird noises and hovering. Maybe a pirate lost him?

Day 1
Day 5
Day 10
Day 15
Day 20
Day 25
Day 30
Day 35
Day 40
Day 45
Day 50

I'm not going mad, no hallucinations, no thoughts of jumping overboard or mad plans and inventions for my return. My hectic brain has chilled. My brother wanted to know if I've found myself! Made me laugh and have yet to tell him that happened long before I set out on this, maybe that's why it's not so so tough. Saying that, I will NOT be doing it again! For someone who loves the company of others and talking, I'm surprisingly content with my waves, little cabin and sore bottom (although I have actually mastered good upkeep of that now): talc, surgical spirit, fresh air and some baseline type shield a friend gave me. Now down to one loo roll so I think I can safely say that unless something mega happens, that will be finished before I will. Fear not though, I have solutions...

Distance travelled today: 31.99 nautical miles
Total travelled 1,501.10 nautical miles.

# DAY 27

### TUESDAY, 27TH FEBRUARY

Today, Tuesday, I am lying resting before my next shift. When I say no wind, I mean mirror calm. It's blissful and boiling! I think the horizon is three miles and there is nothing for $\pi r^2$ miles. It got me thinking of course, how close is the nearest person to me. Angus says there are people in space closer to me than on earth which is a very cool thought. What is the most isolated anyone is, at this point, on the whole of the earth? I am up there in the top ten? Just a thought.

Right, back to the day job. I think these winds, or lack of them, are here for a while so my mega-fast crossing is not looking so mega-fast but I'm still hoping (and on) for that record. Massive thanks to Angus, my weather man, for pointing me in the right direction and getting me to this point so far.

Distance travelled today: 31.80 nautical miles
Total travelled 1,532.90 nautical miles.

Gran Canaria

Day 1
Day 5
Day 10
Day 15
Day 20
Day 25
Day 30
Day 35
Day 40
Day 45
Day 50

Barbados

# MENTAL STRENGTH TRAINING

Something that's not so easy to train for compared with physical. My belief, however, was that life's experiences and my attitude to much of life would help. However, having a really good purpose for the row, would really make a difference. I hooked up with sports psyche Elena Soja, who not only quickly became a good friend but told me: 'Going for a world record isn't purpose. What will make you get through the bad days?'

The girls and women who had paid to be part of the project, the fundraising for King's and proving to myself and others that you really can do whatever you want if you work together, support each other and have purpose, this would be my purpose. And it worked. A few times, when times were tough, I thought of the money, emotion and effort that had gone into my supporters' involvement in my project. As a result of this project I am now a big advocate for 'purpose leads to success'.

Life's experiences can be good, bad or indifferent but regardless, every single one of those teaches us something. Learning how to see the positive is what I see as mental health training - the more you practice the easier it becomes. Then there's energy. How do you remain energetic when it's tough? How do you have the energy to keep going? I believe the less you think about yourself, stop worrying about things you can't control, be honest about who you are, smile, sing and sleep plenty, the more energetic and happier you are! That's not to say there aren't low times, but they become fewer and further between as you learn how to train the brain and your thoughts.

Does my near-death experience make me stronger and less fearful? Probably to some extent, but isn't it a shame that that's what it takes to live your life and not fear the worst.

# DAY 28

### WEDNESDAY, 28TH FEBRUARY

The slog south continues. Hot and slow (into southwesterly winds today) but all made better by seeing this. A flash of iridescent blue and my eyes were on it. Sleeking around me. Defo no cool down dip today! I need my arms and legs to get me back home safely. It gave me the shivers despite the safety of my boat.

In other news I'm told I have now raised £60k for King's. That's pretty impressive and very generous of everyone. One very good reason to keep on slogging. Thanks all.

Distance travelled today: 23.95 nautical miles
Total travelled 1,556.85 nautical miles.

**Gran Canaria**

Day 1
Day 5
Day 10
Day 15
Day 20
Day 25
Day 30
Day 35
Day 40
Day 45
Day 50

**Barbados**

# ANXIETY

Rowing alone in an environment you've never experienced is, I guess, quite a daunting and scary concept. Then why was I not anxious about it? There seemed to be a distinct lack of fear or worry that something could 'go wrong', and if it did, why was it not putting me off?

This was my analysis of the situation:

If Charlie Pitcher and Angus Collins, two very experienced ocean rowers, were endorsing me then it must be okay. Apparently, I was one of two people they thought was 'strong and mental' enough (I tell myself that strong and mental is better than weak and normal!).

What's the worst that can happen? Obviously it's death but statistically this is highly unlikely. We're all dying, it's the only thing guaranteed in our future, so I'd rather die enjoying myself and doing something worthwhile. I also want to die having lived my life and whilst this may carry higher risks, it better than the alternative.

If everything I need is in place, then I have done everything I can. There is no point worrying about things you can't control. It gets you nowhere other than stressed and low in energy. I learnt this on my (first) death bed, when I realised I was totally out of control and therefore all I could do was be me and stay positive.

There is no point pre-empting something bad. Plan for the worst, dream of the best. Have everything in place physically but planning for the worst is a waste of energy.

Fear and worry waste energy. Every time I feel myself getting anxious, I have to take a step back and ask myself: can I do anything about it? If yes, do it; if no, get over it. Eventually you become better at this process and spend less time worrying. Mental health training.

# DAY 29

## THURSDAY, 1ST MARCH

It's 7am UK time (still no idea what this is mid-Atlantic time but it's still dark). I'm in awe of the setting moon in the west and the slight lightening sky in the east and then I hear something. I see something and out of the glassy rolling swell, a pod of dolphins swims with me on their way to wherever. Who gets the opportunity to have dolphins swimming and surfacing in the reflection of a full setting moon? What a way to start week 5.

The past two weeks have gone on forever and I think I have moved about 300 nautical miles in that time. I'm not measuring my daily distance anymore so I've no idea. It's not good for morale! I just have to remember that every stroke is closer and that I will get there. All I remember is thinking that six weeks was definitely achievable. Now I'll be lucky if I do it in seven! It's hot (37 degrees, two knots of wind if I'm lucky) what wind there is is still coming from the west and making what power I do have pretty useless. Even worse, I'm heading south away from this mega system above me (I thank my lucky stars I'm not up there though). Speaking of wind, I think my body produces more than Mother Nature at the moment. Brings a smile to the face if nothing else!

My thoughts are still pretty basic and obscure (no change there then). Today, being as calm as it is, I

Day 1
Day 5
Day 10
Day 15
Day 20
Day 25
Day 30
Day 35
Day 40
Day 45
Day 50

can see tracks on the surface of the water, I presume from passing ships. Now, considering I've seen one ship in five weeks and the closest last Saturday was 260 kilometres away, I wonder when these tracks are from. How long do they last there in the sea and what causes the water to be more glassy where they have passed? I actually rowed down one for a while and considering the scale of this place, that was pretty cool. Simple things, hey!

I am eating my main meals fine and probably about half my snack pack now. Some things I just can't eat but think all is good. My body has adjusted now. I'm sure when I watch some films and series at night and seem to be fixated by the food they are always eating! Take-aways, eating out... I should just be thankful that I have nutritious food but I can't help but dream... first world issues, I know, sorry.

Boat and body maintenance in the middle of the day: I'm pretty excited to have removed a large bag of rubbish from the cabin and can now start afresh. My food seems to go everywhere so finding lots of chilli and pasta in little nooks and crannies. The memory of the shark is still too recent, so the bottom of the boat will have to wait. My balls aren't big enough although probably a bit irrational.

Sunset was as amazing as sunrise except moon and sun in opposite places. Good day but this slow row-ing is definitely affecting the body so I give myself the luxury of a stretch and dig my thumbs hard into my back muscles. All good though.

## *Weather Update*

"Those of you who've been following Kiko's track recently will have seen she's slowed right down and she's been diving south and that's because we've got a westerly wind system to the north. We've been trying to get her away from that which is pushing her in the wrong direction and bring her down into winds which are pointing in the right direction.

At the moment she's here as of 4 o'clock today and this weather is light winds, really horrible and it's swirling around in all directions. If we fast forward over the next 24 hours the winds are generally starting to come more from the east and we will hopefully see that Kiko is further south on Saturday morning and the winds are going to help her along in a  westerly direction. Later on next week she's going to have to fight south-easterly winds pushing her up before the winds get very strong from the east and then it's plain sailing into Barbados.

That explains what we expect to see for Kiko in the next three or four days. Hopefully, the toughest period's almost done and the rest is just more rowing and eating and sleeping."

*Angus Collins*

Distance travelled today: 29.30 nautical miles
Total travelled 1,586.15 nautical miles.

**Gran Canaria**

— Day 1
— Day 5
— Day 10
— Day 15
— Day 20
— Day 25
— Day 30
— Day 35
— Day 40
— Day 45
— Day 50

**Barbados**

# DAY 30

## FRIDAY, 2ND MARCH

Too hot to do much. It takes it out of you. I'm sure my bottle of water has doubled in weight. It's barely worth the effort, so 3pm UK time I'm sitting in my cabin sweating and naked, writing this. I tried to row but thought I'd save my energy for the easterlies on their way tonight! Or at least wait until the sun isn't directly on top of me with no wind. Whatever fashion thing I do, it works for about ten minutes and then its effect wears off. From silk scarfs to wet T-shirt. I have given the bottom of the boat a clean along with a little fish I found sheltering from the sun. Cools me down and cleans me too.

My satellite phone is playing up. You'd think in this day and age of technology Iridium would have developed something a little more reliable. I start to wonder what would happen if I suddenly can't contact Angus. I know it would be fine but should really talk about contingencies. Didn't have enough money for a back-up so I guess I will deal with whatever. I'm sure it will be fine. I mean, I know where I'm going so... (this is not something for people to worry about; if it happens it happens )

I'm afraid this blog is all a bit boring but thank your lucky stars it's only been five minutes of your life and you're not actually living it! I'm fine, but definitely keen to get moving west.

**Gran Canaria**

- Day 1
- Day 5
- Day 10
- Day 15
- Day 20
- Day 25
- Day 30
- Day 35
- Day 40
- Day 45
- Day 50

**Barbados**

I hear you have snow and the UK has come to a standstill too. Trying to think where I'd rather be. It's difficult to know. Think I'm happy enough here. Thinking about my arrival time (how long it takes) and I hope it's enough to get the record but not so great that there aren't some other women out there who are inspired to give it a go. I'm sure that there are plenty of girls and women who could easily do what I will have done and really hope there is a woman number 7, 8, 9, 10 and more, giving it a go in the near future. That would be awesome.

Anyway, I'm going to sleep so I can row tonight in the cool of the full moon. Thanks as always for messages. I do get them and appreciate them, just can't reply to any out here but massive thanks for support.

Distance travelled today: 16.97 nautical miles
Total travelled 1,603.12 nautical miles.

# DAY 31

### SATURDAY, 3RD MARCH

I can't remember much about today and one day is now blurring into the next. All I remember is that it's the last day of the no wind/westerlies. I'm pretty excited. Two weeks ago I was talking about there being three weeks left. I'm still talking about there being three weeks left and I'm now entering week five and was hoping I'd be somewhere nearing the home straight but I just have to take each shift as it comes.

I desalinate the sea water every day (I told an audience once that I had slowly trained myself to drink salt water and had adapted my body; they believed me but quickly realised I was teasing when I told them I had a machine that converted sea water to cider). Reverse osmosis I think? I usually fill a couple of water bottles and my sports ones. I'm not a big drinker so it lasts a while. If the watermaker died a death I have some reserve and a hand pump which I've been told you sweat more pumping than you make! Sounds great. So, fingers crossed the electric one doesn't break. The wind's changed, yes, and some miles were made but not many. The wind is SE so now pushing me north west back to the system I'm trying to avoid. Brilliant!

Distance travelled today: 42.14 nautical miles
Total travelled 1,645.26 nautical miles.

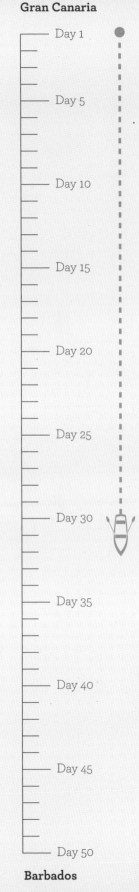

Day 1
Day 5
Day 10
Day 15
Day 20
Day 25
Day 30
Day 35
Day 40
Day 45
Day 50

# LONELINESS

I'm often asked how I coped with loneliness in such a massive open space as the Atlantic Ocean. But loneliness is not about being alone. It's an emotion caused by fear of being left alone involuntarily, not accepted and not being loved. I don't have any of these and haven't felt lonely for several years. My mind can certainly entertain me as well. I had so much support at home that I was never really alone.

I also enjoyed the silence. I'd been so busy planning and fundraising for King's and the project before setting out that I needed a break from all that. I think my perspective on life is already where I want it to be and nothing has really changed there.

I did feel pretty insignificant relative to the ocean. I used to love standing in the boat and looking around, seeing nothing but a vast expanse of ocean and thinking 'Wow, just wow!' So much space and no one else around. It was pretty exhilarating and weird to think that there was no one for hundreds of miles around. The astronauts in space were often closer to me than anyone on Earth.

# DAY 32

### SUNDAY, 4TH MARCH

Lost the will to live twice today. Sun came up, couldn't get the boat moving in the right direction at a sensible speed and started to wonder why I was being tested. All I asked for was some normal decent winds and I get everything else. Have been so excited to start moving again and now my boat feels like a lead balloon in treacle.

I'm sitting here wondering if the couple of miles is worth the effort and I am questioning my strength. It's gusty so my boat changes direction the whole time and I'm trying to stop it going north (I stopped using the autopilot after week 1 so I'm operating the rudder manually)... Bingo, I figured it out. There is seaweed everywhere and once I realised I had a massive piece stuck on my rudder, it's back to a somewhat relatively easier life. The wind changes slightly and I'm back up to speed. It's all temporary if a little painful at times!

Songs (one liners generally, as I'm rubbish at remembering much more) are sung and positive thoughts return.

Distance travelled today: 49.26 nautical miles
Total travelled 1,694.52 nautical miles.

**Gran Canaria**

Day 1

Day 5

Day 10

Day 15

Day 20

Day 25

Day 30

Day 35

Day 40

Day 45

Day 50

**Barbados**

# SINGLE LIFE

It's one of the first things people ask. We are programmed from such a young age to think we must get married and have kids that we spend so much of our time and effort trying to attract a member of the opposite sex. Unfortunately, as a result, we spend much less time on ourselves. It's a question I never get asked anymore because the answer is always the same! "Still single!" I feel people are more interested in the other things I do, rather than my relationship status.

Mum once told me I was an acquired taste! First Dates (TV dating programme) said they'd struggle to find me someone! But you know what, I don't care. Life on my own has become what I've made it. I have great friends, too many nieces and nephews to count, not a huge amount of time left in the day but more importantly, the 13 years I've been single have really allowed me to become me! I'm so content. Being on your own forces you to survive, to think for yourself and allows you the space to grow and become you. It makes you independent, confident and resilient. I firmly believe that being on your own for a substantial length of time is essential. It takes time to be comfortable with yourself, but once you're there, it's great. Why be with someone who doesn't make you happy or a better person? My happiness comes from the experiences I have with other people, from my experiences, from you. So, if you're single and worried about it, don't be, use the time to know yourself. If you're with someone who doesn't make you a better person or happy, then why bother? And if you're neither of these, then awesome, you're a very lucky person... One day!

# DAY 33

## MONDAY, 5TH MARCH

Much the same as yesterday so thought I'd write about my day, my 'routine' so to speak. Now, I'm not one for routine; in fact I hate constraints and lack of flexibility. This may have caused me issues in 'getting into a routine' early on, but perhaps it has allowed me to 'enjoy' my journey a bit more. No idea. I do however, try to make sure I'm out rowing for at least 12 hours a day but when I put the hours in is dictated by how I'm feeling rather than a rule I've set myself in advance.

Let's say the day starts at 6.30am. It's dark and probably more like 4.30am local time but I've stuck to UK time for ease. Sometimes I'm up at 5.30 pottering, having breakfast (large portion of muesli mix thing and dried fruit I made before leaving), contemplating going back to sleep, chatting to my video diary (kept me sane without a doubt, but I pity the production crew who will have to listen to the inner thoughts of Kiko!). I'll do two hours rowing, normally bringing me to sunrise. From then on in, I have now settled into two hours on and 30-40 mins off, so that by midnight depending on how I feel (sometimes this is 10.30pm or maybe even 2.00am) I am done for the day and I go to bed. Most often with the intention of getting back up to row more but have found my body is dead and can't move

Day 1

Day 5

Day 10

Day 15

Day 20

Day 25

Day 30

Day 35

Day 40

Day 45

Day 50

(at this point I weigh up the benefits of sleep over miles!). Generally, sleep wins. Naughty and I have a mental guilt battle with myself about whether I'm being lazy; if I have earned it or if my body really is that paralysed that I must have more zeds.

In my breaks I power nap, check emails, write my blog (I lose sleep to keep you updated so hope you are appreciating and enjoying), tidy the boat, wash some clothes, clean the bottom of the boat, phone Angus for weather updates, clean and air my bottom (TMI!) and then it's time to get back out. I eat on the go. It's an opportunity to have a one minute break (maybe this is optimistic?), stand and shake my poor withering body (definitely more fat than muscle now - will be looking half athlete, half slob by the time I arrive!) and make some water. I row while filling a bottle or two for the day ahead.

And that's it. While I sleep, the boat does its thing and hopefully, when the wind is good, it blows me in the right direction with some speed but as you'll all know, this hasn't been the case for a lot of the time so sometimes I barely go anywhere or in a less than ideal direction. It can also take a good few minutes of my snooze time to figure out the best rudder and daggerboard combination to get it all setup. Painful when all I want to do is snooze. Sometimes I'm naughty and anticipate this time and take it out of rowing time. Maybe that's why I'm behind schedule!

I think that's it. Pretty simple, boring and monotonous. After every two hours I long for the little break but knowing that I have another and another and another and another (you get the picture), it's a wonder how one mentally carries on, but then I look around and realise there's not much else to do and no other choice really! No bus stops or distractions so another shift it will be. 5pm is sweetie time and at night I have my iPad for some series and film viewing - both help massively.

One day at a time, one shift at a time, one stroke at a time. I'm getting there (hoping for a 49 day arrival now so fingers crossed, a world record and first solo woman under 50 days... but life never goes to plan so let's see!

Distance travelled today: 56.24 nautical miles
Total travelled 1,750.76 nautical miles.

**Gran Canaria**

Day 1

Day 5

Day 10

Day 15

Day 20

Day 25

Day 30

Day 35

Day 40

Day 45

Day 50

**Barbados**

# MEDICATION

Rowing the Atlantic is a very physical and mentally stressful endurance challenge. I was monitoring the signs consistently, looking out for aches, fatigue, sickness, shivering (sounds like all the regular symptoms of rowing an ocean!) and dosing up accordingly. Since my operation, I am now severely deficient in cortisol, one of the four major life sustaining hormones in our bodies. It is released in response to physical and mental stress. Without this hormone, I would probably die within five days, but manage it daily through meds ... Being physically sick, or accidents, bumps, breaks and things such as capsizes would require an emergency boost to replicate what would naturally happen in my body. It's all very achievable if I'm sensible and aware, but it adds a little extra spice to the whole challenge. Fortunately, a degree in molecular biology helps as does the desire to live!

When I was at King's College Hospital before setting out, we went through how to make and administer this so that I could then ram the needle in my thigh with a mega dose. What was also pretty cool was that King's wanted me to record data as there is nothing out there related to my condition (secondary adrenal insufficiency) and such a massive endurance exercise. Great to think that this could lead to some interesting qualitative data and something for other people with the disease to look at as to what is possible for them.

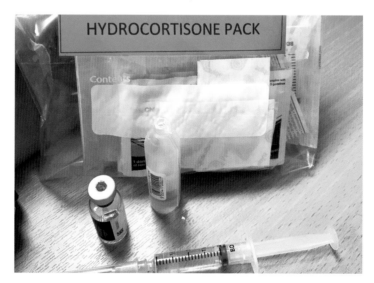

# DAY 34

TUESDAY, 6TH MARCH

First things first: at midnight I made the 1,000 nautical miles to go point! Whoop, whoop!

Winds are here and those following me should see an improvement now. I've set my sights on trying to make Barbados in under 50 days which I think requires about 61 nautical miles a day. That's a good amount to cover so the challenge is certainly not done yet. Suddenly I am realising how every mile really does count and every ten minutes off the oars (and faffing!) makes a big difference so I'm becoming stricter with myself. So much time wasted early on.

I'm now constantly hungry which is good but not sure if I'm eating all that I'm expending, and some of it just really doesn't go down well. But happy on the nutrition front. On the medication front I'm feeling 10,000,000 times better and can make it through the day without constantly thinking about sleep.

**Gran Canaria**

Day 1
Day 5
Day 10
Day 15
Day 20
Day 25
Day 30
Day 35
Day 40
Day 45
Day 50

**Barbados**

Two boats radioed me in the last 24 hours, both wondering what a 20ft boat was doing and whether I needed anything. A coffee and Club biscuit would have been nice. Felt good to know I was being looked after and spotted their boats too. First sign of humans in 34 days (except for the plastic floating - Grrrrr).

I'm still amazes me that I can get out of my cabin and row another two hours, staring at yet more ocean with only my mind for entertainment. The amount of times I have played over my arrival is ridiculous... and the fresh food, clean clothes, mojito, bed and shower!

Distance travelled today: 58.48 nautical miles
Total travelled 1,809.24 nautical miles.

# DAY 35

WEDNESDAY, 7TH MARCH

It seems windy but I'm not really going anywhere fast. I like to understand why and hate doing things wrong so the idea that I haven't got it right really frustrates me and it still all baffles me but you have to go with what you got. Anyway, here's for the night shift.

I force myself up, and turn into a childish version of baby pose, like I'm crying into my pillow (!) and have words with myself: 'Kiko, you can't keep making excuses for not getting out, you won't make it in two weeks with that attitude!' I'm a little nervous of the dark and the waves, especially since I got soaked by a rogue side wave just an hour before, but I realise I'm right; I'll be here forever if I don't just get over it and get out. It's 11.30pm and I start my shift. After about 30 minutes my eyeballs start rolling and I'm falling asleep.

**Gran Canaria**

Day 1

Day 5

Day 10

Day 15

Day 20

Day 25

Day 30

Day 35

Day 40

Day 45

Day 50

**Barbados**

Every stroke is a huge effort. Is it worth the effort? Then I remember I have pills! Caffeine, Vitb2 and some CurraNZ (black currant lifesavers). Within about 30 minutes I'm on top of the world.

Phosphorescence sparkles like stars and the occasional flash, like someone is taking photos from the deep; my eyesight adjusts and I'm in the zone. Actually I'm really loving it and thinking I could go on forever but my two hours is up and I should get some sleep. 1.30 am end. Shift two, 90 minutes later, is less of a mental battle. I know what to expect and I'm happy. I'm rowing, looking from side to side in wonder of it all and then, all of a sudden, my chilli pork scratchings and bag start going crazy! They've come alive! It takes a few seconds to realise, when I hear a load of frantic flapping, what has just happened. A poor old flying fish made a beeline for the wrong landing. I have to say, they are pretty cool, but I'm not sure they have mastered their landing style quite yet. Bit scrappy! I rescue him and throw him into the air - I'm not 100% sure this had the desired effect. Had kind of half hoped he'd fly off into the distance; instead it landed with a thud. It looked (as much as I could see in the dark) that he just lay there. Probably got chilli on his wings.

Shift three, 6am-8am, still dark as this is UK time. Same good feelings and moon is in full swing lighting up the sky. It's rising about 3am GMT and a welcome relief when it's there. Suddenly I see massive glowing jellyfish. I think! 3ft x 1ft and globular. Very cool! By 8am I'm ready for a rest, the caffeine has worked off and I retreat to my home, pleased with myself for doing 5½ hours before sunrise - normal for a team of ocean rowers but not for me (I have 30 minutes off between day shifts, they have two hours). Gold stars all round! 45 minutes sleep and then it's the start of the day shift. No rest for the wicked.

For such a boring and simple existence, days go very quickly and already I'm confused where one of my days has gone (writing the blog in batches, trying to remember!). I assume this means nothing significant happened. I did see a big yellow and blue striped fish and I have a few tiddlers following me now. I guess we're moving into tropical fish now.

Storm petrel still here and frequenting a little more often. Dad says she will leave me soon as will not be wanting to end up in Barbados. I say, if it's my Grandma then she'll come the whole way. Would be mean not to! Otherwise it's headed south soon. Maybe she's spending more time with me cos she's saying goodbye! Petrel comes from St Peter. My grandmother was a staunch Catholic, so quite apt.

Distance travelled today: 48.17 nautical miles
Total travelled 1,857.41 nautical miles.

Day 1
Day 5
Day 10
Day 15
Day 20
Day 25
Day 30
Day 35
Day 40
Day 45
Day 50

# WHAT IF IT ALL GOES WRONG?

It's pretty hard for it all to go wrong. But it could! I could have got ill, I could have hated it, hit a submerged container, could have capsized with the cabin door open and the electrics could have all died. Could, could, could… They were all very unlikely especially if I did what I was meant to, but sometimes things are uncontrollable.

So, what if I needed or wanted out? The EPIRB is a big handheld device which you can activate and a message gets sent to Falmouth. They will try to make contact, assess the issue and then send the nearest boat to you for a rescue. It is international shipping law that a distress call must be answered, and this can take days to happen. Once you are out of helicopter flying distance, this is your only hope. If something happens to the boat and it's sinking there is a life-raft. You don't leave the boat unless it's sinking. I had training in this but it's so heavy I wondered if I'd actually have managed to chuck it overboard. There's also a 'grab bag' that you take with this, containing some water, GPS, food, flares etc. and you would definitely take the EPIRB with you as well. However, this only lasts 48 hours so, attached to the lifejacket (which I never wore), is a PLB (a personal smaller version of the EPIRB) which emits a signal for another 24 hours. There's obviously the Yellowbrick tracker (that was used throughout the trip) if you had time to detach from the boat. If you go overboard without being strapped in you're pretty much saying goodbye to life, so it became standard practice to clip in and out when exiting and entering the cabin. I value my life a little bit! So, all in all, death was pretty unlikely!

*Image courtesy of Ocean Signal*

# DAY 36

## THURSDAY, 8TH MARCH

The winds are picking up, I'm getting excited! Aim now is for at least 65 nautical miles consistently to make sure I comfortably make 49 if not 48 days. There's a lot of £££ pledged to King's College for each day under the record so it's in my interest to go quickly, as well as the fresh food, white sheets and mojitos!

I have a very random thought of settling down and having babies! Seems a far more sensible idea than rowing oceans. Haven't had thoughts of babies since I was engaged in 2005. The ocean is making me go mad! Then I have another thought: what if this crossing was just the practice? Perhaps I should go again but with everything I want and need on the boat and it actually being useful. Knowing what to expect etc. I then combine the two ideas, and decide if I do get to having sprogs, which I will need to get a move on if I do, we could do a family holiday ocean crossing. How many kids (not sure what age they'd have to be) could say they had rowed the Atlantic with their parents before they'd left school? Count your lucky stars I'm not your Mum. No Centre Parks or Butlins in the (imaginary) Kiko household. Actually I quite like the idea, so next step, find a man who agrees it sounds fun.

Gran Canaria

Day 1
Day 5
Day 10
Day 15
Day 20
Day 25
Day 30
Day 35
Day 40
Day 45
Day 50
Barbados

So have I gone mad, is the question? Has life at sea alone got the better of me? I feel the same but when there is nothing to distract you, no job, no friends, no news, no meetings, no shopping, it allows your brain to explore. I have been genuinely mad (from the Cushings') and it's not much fun when you realise the thoughts you are having or things you've said aren't rational. People judge, yet it's out of your control. These thoughts though (of family crossings) are just fun ideas, picking up on simple observations or thoughts and running with it, allowing the brain to have a bit of fun and with there being no distractions to stop it, I guess they happen more easily. Anyway, they are keeping me entertained so I don't really care. Mad, I may be.

My few body niggles are coming a bit more than they're going now, mostly my hands and wrists. My legs are definitely getting more pathetic and I can noticeably tell that I've been rowing a while. But with only a short time left I'm pretty sure I'll cope - it's amazing that I've got this far without anything too debilitating or painful.

So, I think that's it. I'm not sure how I manage to write so much with so little going on but there you have it. Hope you can find pleasure from something small and have the space to allow your mind to wander so you can wonder. It's fun.

Distance travelled today: 59.37 nautical miles
Total travelled 1,916.78 nautical miles.

# DAY 37

## FRIDAY, 9TH MARCH

I just can't get over how quickly time flies. There was me once again thinking I only had two days to write and realise there's today's too... and already I've forgotten what happened! I guess it's because there is so little happening to distinguish between the days that they all seem the same. It's all waves, rowing, eating, sleeping. Eat, sleep, row, repeat.

Apart from some deep philosophical chat, only suitable in a cosy pub with log fire, I don't have much to report. I am simply on row two hours, stop for 30 minutes, eat some food at various points, power nap (which I have to say I am a bit of a pro at) and row for another two hours. Come midnight I check my miles and bed down for some hours until it all starts again. Can't believe I've been doing this now for 38 days? It's just become life and both body and mind are well adjusted now. Saying that, I wouldn't mind the odd change now and again! I think I did a big day on the miles. Maybe 70+ nautical miles (80 car miles) - happy with that as I worked to get it!

Distance travelled today: 57.87 nautical miles
Total travelled 1,974.65 nautical miles.

Gran Canaria

Day 1
Day 5
Day 10
Day 15
Day 20
Day 25
Day 30
Day 35
Day 40
Day 45
Day 50

# MY EQUIPMENT

**Para-Anchor** – like a big parachute that you deploy and sits underwater, preventing you going in the direction of the wind (or very slowly at least).

**Autopilot** – I only used this at the start and end, otherwise I hand steered. This controls the direction and you have to swap over on a regular basis as they overheat (not designed for ocean rowing speeds).

**First Aid** – All sorts and I only used the TCP for my bottom!

**Watermaker** – Converts sea water to fresh. Gobbles up battery power.

**Life Raft** – Thankfully never used!

**Gas Bag & Flares** – for life raft and rescue.

**Food** – 50 days of dried meals and snack packs.

**EPIRP** – The safety button.

Plus a load of other rubbish I thought I'd need and never used.

# DAY 38

### SATURDAY, 10TH MARCH

Pretty much the same as yesterday. The bloody seaweed is doing my head in as it gets stuck on the rudder and takes ages to fall off (five minutes or so) and in the meantime the boat seems to double in weight. I've named the last of the leg 'mile munching' as if I put the miles in the days will disappear, rather than trying to figure out when I'll arrive (hoping a week Thursday morning so I make it in under seven weeks).

Little goals really motivate me and I can see now that every hour I row is one hour sooner that I arrive. CANNOT WAIT! Can't believe I've actually gone and done this! (Touch wood). It was just some slight off the cuff idea that currently has me getting a world record and raising £62k for the hospital that saved my life (and a lot more pledged still to come). Madness! I'm a Taurus - like a bull in a china shop: do or say something and deal with the consequences after. This idea is looking like it may have worked out ok

Distance travelled today: 69.33 nautical miles
Total travelled 2,043.98 nautical miles.

**Gran Canaria**

Day 1
Day 5
Day 10
Day 15
Day 20
Day 25
Day 30
Day 35
Day 40
Day 45
Day 50

**Barbados**

# WILDLIFE

You'd think that wildlife was everywhere in the Atlantic, and it probably is... metres below the surface where I can't see anything. There was actually so little that a seagull would have been exciting; even seeing a small fish would make my day! I loved watching the birds swooping and playing in the waves, the fish following me in my slipstream and the dolphins playing around the boat. But the top seven memorable wildlife moments were:

1. The white whale of which I am told there are only four in the world.
2. The whale surfing down the wave coming straight at me, turning slightly at the last minute, slowing then rolling on to its side and looking directly at me.
3. The storm petrel following and visiting me every day.
4. The flying fish bouncing off my chin.
5. The dolphins quietly going on their way, gently puffing and splashing past the boat in the dark of night, the moon setting on one side, sun starting to rise on the other.
6. A young bird hitching a ride for 18 hours on the back of the boat.
7. And, of course, the shark slinking around me. Weirdly, even though I was in my boat, the hairs on my neck still stood on end.

Other than the odd email or text, the wildlife really was the only thing that was exciting. It would really brighten up my shift or even day just seeing something out there. When you're totally alone, it's weird how anything living becomes company, becomes a 'being' rather than just another animal. I also felt I was on their turf (what's the water version of this phrase?) rather than on land where humans clearly are in charge. I felt an equal

# DAY 39

## SUNDAY, 11TH MARCH

I was wondering what to write today. Same waves, same wind, same good and bad things (there aren't many of either) and then this massive brown long thing came careering towards me down a wave. A whale surfing at the speed of light (exaggeration) two metres from the boat. It must be said, I was a little scared and excited at the same time! I thought it was a killer whale (desperately want to see one of these) until I saw another one, and another and realised in fact it wasn't. Any guesses on 30-40ft long, brown with white underneath at front? Three in total, uber happy days!

And as if that wasn't enough, an hour later a pod of about, I reckon, 30 dolphins came and played around my boat. Totally awesome.

Distance travelled today: 70.64 nautical miles
Total travelled 2,114,.62 nautical miles.

**Gran Canaria**

Day 1
Day 5
Day 10
Day 15
Day 20
Day 25
Day 30
Day 35
Day 40
Day 45
Day 50

**Barbados**

103

# DAY 40

## MONDAY, 12TH MARCH

Started well today and the mile munching is coming along nicely with nearly 10 nautical miles down in two hours (this is speedy!). It's pretty much perfect conditions and at this rate I'll be in Barbados in nine days. Feeling strong, all the mini aches and pains seem to have subsided, even the bottom is playing ball (I picked all the little spots and it seems to have done the trick! Released the pressure and made a world of difference. Never agreed with the 'don't pick spots' policy!)

It's now 10pm and I should have another shift before I settle for my longer sleep but I'm rewarding myself. I'm tired and will have rowed/travelled (as the crow flies so more in reality) 73 nautical miles closer to Barbados so I'm rewarding myself with moisturising my body (needs it!), cutting my toenails, drinking my last bottle of Coca-Cola and having a couple of extra hours zzzzz.

Annoyingly, because I am hand-steering and not using my autopilot (I prefer hand steering, that's all. Pros and cons of both), I have to check the boat is on course about every 30 minutes. As a master of 30 minute snoozing, I guess it's not the end of the world that it's interrupted sleep.

Gran Canaria

Day 1
Day 5
Day 10
Day 15
Day 20
Day 25
Day 30
Day 35
Day 40
Day 45
Day 50

Barbados

Anyway, I think that's it from the Atlantic. I haven't seen the storm petrel for a couple of days. She/it did an unusual dive bomb on my head and perhaps this was its farewell. However, I have had a few visits from the cool white tropical-looking seagull so maybe that's taken over!

Think we're looking at a Wednesday, 21st, evening or Thursday, 22nd, arrival! So exciting - eeeek. World record, fresh food and clean bed and clothes. Touch wood! If you know anyone in Barbados, please let them know or get booking tickets now!

Distance travelled today: 73.41 nautical miles
Total travelled 2,188,.03 nautical miles.

# DAY 41

### TUESDAY, 13TH MARCH

No idea once again what happened today. It's too far away to remember amongst a sea of nothingness, quite literally. I have stopped listening to music podcasts and watching stuff on my iPad as I seem capable of getting through shifts without them. I'm still amazed by the fact I continue to get up out of my cabin and row for two hours, again and again and again. I don't really have a choice, I know, but it is odd. Oh, and the storm petrel is back. Not sure when it'll make its turn off south but he/she hasn't got long! We're estimating a Wednesday 21st evening arrival if I can keep up my average of three knots. Exciting!

Distance travelled today: 70.57 nautical miles
Total travelled 2,258,.60 nautical miles.

Day 1
Day 5
Day 10
Day 15
Day 20
Day 25
Day 30
Day 35
Day 40
Day 45
Day 50

Barbados

# DAY 42

## WEDNESDAY, 14TH MARCH

There I am, standing at the cabin door about to go inside after almost getting my satellite phone off my outdoor contraption (the indoor aerial has stopped working so I have to go outside and wait around for messages and emails, and it's no 4G, I assure you). Anyway, standing, fortunately holding on, when out of nowhere, the most massive rogue wave comes from the side and the next thing I know I'm hanging out of the boat holding on for (not quite) dear life! The boat is amazingly designed and struggles to flip right over so I'm very lucky. A little wobbly and very thankful that (a) the satphone has survived (it's my only form of communication with UK) and (b) it wasn't 30 seconds later when I was opening the cabin door and (c) it wasn't two minutes earlier when I was sitting on my bucket mid poo! It taught me that, just because you're nearly there and you're well accustomed to what the sea has to offer, you can never have a day off from safety and that the ocean is defo the boss. Spilt my bloody muesli everywhere again. It's the bane of my life. I added linseed and chia which constantly get engrained into my already sore bottom because they somehow make their way into the small sheepskin I sit on. Simple pleasures like a bowl and table wouldn't go amiss!

Distance travelled today: 70.69 nautical miles
Total travelled 2,329,.29 nautical miles.

**Gran Canaria**

Day 1
Day 5
Day 10
Day 15
Day 20
Day 25
Day 30
Day 35
Day 40
Day 45
Day 50

**Barbados**

# FOOD

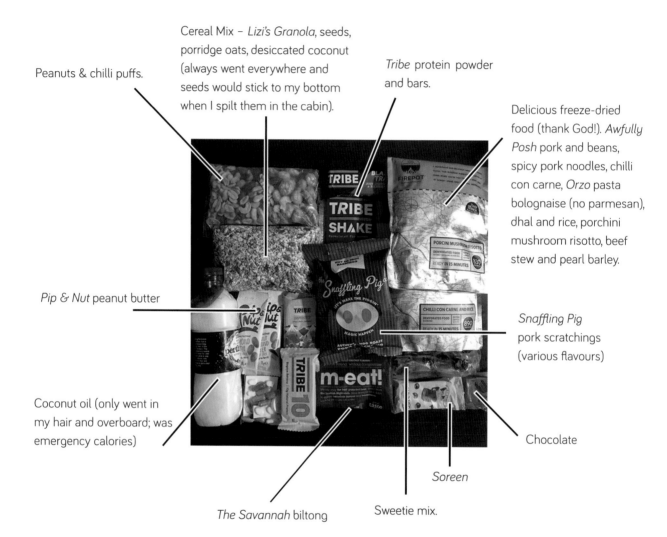

Peanuts & chilli puffs.

Cereal Mix – *Lizi's Granola*, seeds, porridge oats, desiccated coconut (always went everywhere and seeds would stick to my bottom when I spilt them in the cabin).

*Tribe* protein powder and bars.

Delicious freeze-dried food (thank God!). *Awfully Posh* pork and beans, spicy pork noodles, chilli con carne, *Orzo* pasta bolognaise (no parmesan), dhal and rice, porchini mushroom risotto, beef stew and pearl barley.

*Pip & Nut* peanut butter

*Snaffling Pig* pork scratchings (various flavours)

Coconut oil (only went in my hair and overboard; was emergency calories)

Chocolate

*Soreen*

*The Savannah* biltong

Sweetie mix.

# DAY 43

### THURSDAY, 15TH MARCH

Winds are decreasing. Boo. Bit disheartening when you're nearly there and another curveball is chucked your way. I was beginning to smell the food, feel the fresh sheets (everything I have is sticky, damp and salty), taste the mojito and hear the sound of humans. It puts my arrival back by probably a day, depending on how hard I push myself. On one side of the coin I have now fully adapted to a life of rowing and ocean, but on the other, I am feeling the strain on my body... my point being, I'm not sure how much more I can push at this stage.

I see a boat in the dark. It's a small sailing boat, two nautical miles away. Maybe a solo or a couple of guys. It looks like it's coming to say hi. I start to get emotional as I haven't seen another human for 43 days. Maybe I'll invite him on board. Perhaps I should tidy up and make myself look nice. Maybe he's hot. Maybe I should radio. I'm nervous in case... I don't know. They seem to be moving closer... they'll radio, then they go back to the original course and on they go. Sad. Then I go into the cabin, only to see I have accidentally nudged my radio onto channel 17 (it should be on channel 16) so they were probably trying but I never replied. Husband number 432 missed opportunity!

Distance travelled today: 64.83 nautical miles
Total travelled 2,394.12 nautical miles.

Gran Canaria

— Day 1

— Day 5

— Day 10

— Day 15

— Day 20

— Day 25

— Day 30

— Day 35

— Day 40

— Day 45

— Day 50

Barbados

# MY EN SUITE BATHROOM

I'm often asked about toileting while at sea. (I'm aware it's not for everyone, so if you don't want to know, maybe skip this bit)...

Basically, I had a bucket (the most annoying bit of equipment as it has no real home and even by the end, was getting in the way). I would put one piece of kitchen roll on the bottom, sit, poo and chuck overboard, clean and that was it. Simple when the weather was good, a little more hairy when rough. To wee, I would stand with a measuring jug clamped between my legs (donated by King's College Hospital Biochemistry Department!) and hold on to the boat. Done, chuck, row.

# DAY 44

## FRIDAY, 16TH MARCH

The last Friday of the challenge, I hope. It's very touch and go with these decreased winds but fingers crossed. I'm trying hard! 14-15 hours rowing and about four-five hours broken sleep. My body is definitely in shut-down mode. Struggling to get out the cabin and everything feels heavy. Lost my appetite because it is so hot (34 degrees in the shade apparently). Unfortunately these gentle winds are a bit of a setback but there's nothing I can do, out of my control, and every row stroke is one step closer, so on I plod.

For some reason, I always look over my left arm and today this huge (40-50ft) white whale (really?) came right up to the surface. It was not a hallucination, I promise! I always say hello to my animals in the hope they speak a little human but this beast had done all he wanted and dived back down. Any ideas on what species this would be and if I was mistaken?

Sorry, blogs are coming a bit few and far between. It's either writing or sleeping and often sleeping takes precedence.

Distance travelled today: 65.56 nautical miles
Total travelled 2,459.68 nautical miles.

Day 1

Day 5

Day 10

Day 15

Day 20

Day 25

Day 30

Day 35

Day 40

Day 45

Day 50

# NUTRITION

I'm not one for following plans or sticking to rules. 'You must eat like this and train like that'... Really?

The truth:... Nutrition in the run up to the challenge consisted largely of Club biscuits and coffee for breakfast, cheese and ham sandwiches for lunch and sometimes something a bit more substantial for dinner. I believe life is for enjoying so if there happens to be a pub halfway on a bike ride or paddle session, then I stop. I had a few issues with my post-surgery diet and lost a fair amount of weight, but once the medication was sorted, I quickly returned to normal.

On the boat, it was all dried food. Lots of protein and calories. I'd been advised that I would burn 6,000 calories a day so that is what I packed for: 50 days of food, including snacks and main meals. I couldn't eat for the first two and a half weeks or the last week because it was so hot and as a result I lost about seven kilos. My boobs and bum disappeared, as did my calves, tummy and thighs so I imagine that's where a lot of the calories were coming off.! I actually returned with 26 days of food.

I've never taken a vitamin in my life and had a few people kindly offer me their miracle health supplements that, embarrassingly, I could never tell any difference when taking. They didn't last. The only thing I swore by, and used all the way across the Atlantic, were CurraNZ – blackcurrant capsules that reduced aches and increased performance. Considering I broke the record and had no significant aches or pains for 3,000 miles, I'd say they did what they claimed!

# DAY 45

## SATURDAY, 17TH MARCH

Early am: 'Should have gone to spec savers'. Luckily nothing more than a mix up between stars and cargo ships! All good, but had me worried for a short time. Pitch black and a bright double star (my astigmatism makes me see double at night) rising over my left shoulder. Or is it? I check the chart plotter and no ship to be seen. I check the lights; now there's one it must be a star. No, there are clearly two. My knowledge of ships and lights are that the big ones have two on, one higher than the other, and my intelligence says if sometimes I see one and other times two, this must mean it's somewhat close to either coming straight at me or going away. I start to freak out. It's fine, it's a star, it's not on the chart plotter. I continue to row. Anyway, it turns out I do need to get my appointment booked and buy myself some glasses as it was indeed a ship! 900ft going in the opposite direction. Phew!

Slow, boring winds, taking away all the enjoyment of a speedy delivery to Barbados. Once again, the ocean and weather are testing my patience. Annoying, as family are waiting to welcome me but as for the rest of the trip, it's been pretty inconsistent. Getting slightly bored of its fun.

38 degrees outside and when there's no wind, daytime rowing is absolute hell so I'm trying to

Day 1
Day 5
Day 10
Day 15
Day 20
Day 25
Day 30
Day 35
Day 40
Day 45
Day 50

switch to night rowing, although I don't trust myself to make it through the night without accidentally sleeping through my alarms, so I soldier on through the heat of the day, knowing there's not long. Barbados is in sight (metaphorically speaking!)

Loo roll close to finish so I'd better speed up fast!

Distance travelled today: 56.79 nautical miles
Total travelled 2,516.47 nautical miles.

Photo: Anthony Ball Photography

# DAY 46

## SUNDAY, 18TH MARCH

Row, eat, sleep, although too much of the first and not enough of the other two! Really enjoying seeing the miles disappearing although news that this weather is set to stay for another 48 hours is a little painful. And OMG, the seaweed! You can tell when it's on the rudder as the boat becomes so heavy. Now for the decision to stop rowing and wait for a wave from behind to dislodge it, then start again; this could of course be at any minute or it may even just dislodge itself anyway. Or, do I get off my seat, take off my visor and in a display of all body parts everywhere, grab my little stick and lean over the side/back of the boat, legs splayed, holding on (for dear life would be a slight exaggeration, but it's definitely not the most comfortable position), and try to dislodge anything that's down there?

Either I imagine it or my body is getting considerably, and intermittently, weaker, as there's often nothing there. Sometimes I've been so convinced, I have stuck my snorkel on and plunged my head in as well. It's actually a welcome relief from the heat so not too much of an issue. But I tell you, there's nothing more satisfying than releasing the 'little bugger'! And then back to some slightly easier rowing.

Life on board is becoming noticeably salty and sticky. Everything is a bit crispy or slimy or sticky,

Day 1
Day 5
Day 10
Day 15
Day 20
Day 25
Day 30
Day 35
Day 40
Day 45
Day 50

passenger Kiko included. Time for a shower (in four days? Amazing). And the body is also becoming noticeably more worn and sore. My hands, when I stop or first get on and then sometimes during, are so stiff and sore. I think it's called claw hand from gripping. Made particularly worse because I'm hand steering. I tend to pull a few hard strokes on one side to turn the boat. This requires a good grip but has (nearly) detrimental effects on little bones and muscles in my hands and wrists. The pain thing I've noticed is funny. It's like your body only wants to focus on one pain at a time and so they all come and go and I'd say I was generally in good flabby shape. From muscle to splodge in 48 days! I'm interested to know how much I weigh (was 72kg when I left). And my bottom isn't less sore. My nice new comfortable seat soon became less comfortable and spots have returned. So small, yet so painful. And who on earth thought that bone that sticks out when you sit would make a good evolutionary trait? I want a booty please!

Distance travelled today: 61.14 nautical miles
Total travelled 2,577.61 nautical miles.

# DAY 47

## MONDAY, 19TH MARCH

Mini melt down this morning. Woke up to find the boat was going NW and I wasn't aware this was happening. My parents have kindly booked my tickets home, 24 hours after I arrive. 49 days at sea to get to Barbados and then I'm being whisked home to the snow, just hours later. Not the plan. Back home, I'm pretty much in charge and in control of my life. Out here, it's hard, as everyone else is doing everything for me. I have no choice but to relinquish everything, but it can be frustrating when people don't do things how you'd like or would expect. And it's made even worse by three hours of sleep and nothing else in my life to consider. Poor Angus (weather man) got the brunt of my grumpiness and maybe some tears! Weather still rubbish although it's meant to be improving tomorrow. CANNOT WAIT!

Got hit on the chin by a flying fish. Have rescued six, trodden on one (dead, I hope) and buried seven. Storm petrel still around and did this weird, very close to my head, flying thing again at night. I thought he/she was meant to be migrating south. Seems it'll come all the way, literally. And very cool.

Distance travelled today: 51.79 nautical miles
Total travelled 2,629.40 nautical miles.

Gran Canaria

— Day 1
— Day 5
— Day 10
— Day 15
— Day 20
— Day 25
— Day 30
— Day 35
— Day 40
— Day 45
— Day 50

Barbados

# ENTERTAINMENT ON BOARD

Going solo is never going to be fun. No one to cheer you up, no one to talk to and no one to make you laugh. But, with the wonders of technology, I managed to ward off the brain monsters and kept myself going through the long nights and hot days.

Let's not even go there with my music choice. I'm not sure what made me think I wanted 100 or more classical hits or the greatest power ballads, either. Half my music hadn't downloaded, and the half was rubbish. Saying that, 'This Girl is on Fiyyyyaaaaa' frequently got sung at the top of my voice (I even checked no one was listening once!) and a bit too much *Les Miserables,* but all in all I probably skipped more tunes than listened the full way through.

As for other entertainment, Tom Hardy in the BBC 1 *Taboo* helped me through a few of the calmer dark and lonely nights – ha! But I wouldn't watch anything when I needed to see the waves as the screen caused night blindness, meaning I got wet more often then I'd like. I also wasn't 100% sure on the waterproofness of my case.

And then for the podcasts: *Desert Island Discs* kept me well entertained as did the top selling podcast *My Dad Wrote a Porno* which isn't quite what it sounds like but is hysterically funny/awkward/wrong but highly recommended (if you're of a suitable age). I was particularly upset when I realised I'd only downloaded two random episodes of series 3 though, just as it was getting really good! (Don't judge me on my choice of listening until you have listened yourself – I highly recommend)

Come week six, all my media started running out which was quite fortunate because suddenly I became happy with nothing. My brain had relaxed and endless staring at waves and my own imagination became more than enough for entertainment purposes.

# DAY 48

## TUESDAY, 20TH MARCH

I've no idea what happened today, but it had something to do with the autopilot breaking, seaweed and muesli spilling. Pain in the arse day. So close to home. Feel like pulling the plug but realise it was only because I was worried about everyone coming to Barbados and me being late. They've spent so much money coming to see me, I don't want to be late ... but I remember I can't control the weather. It is what it is.

Distance travelled today: 65.34 nautical miles
Total travelled 2,694.74 nautical miles.

Gran Canaria

Day 1
Day 5
Day 10
Day 15
Day 20
Day 25
Day 30
Day 35
Day 40
Day 45
Day 50

Barbados

Photo: Anthony Ball Photography

# DAY 49

## WEDNESDAY, 21ST MARCH

I decide to hand steer from the cabin while I rest. The boat won't stay on the 254° course I need. I'm up all night, with the ropes fed through a small gap in the cabin hatch. Near the hinge the ropes are pinched tight but near the opening I can pull on them and the rudder and the back of the boat moves.

Suddenly, out of nowhere, a wave hits the boat from the wrong direction and makes its way through the gap, cascading into my dry cabin where most of the water hits the electrics panel. I quickly secure the hatch on full lock, give up on steering and soak up the water. How can this happen so close to the end? Arghh.

Unbelievable. I have no choice now but to row to keep the boat on course. I'm not having that again. But no sleep yet so will just have to keep on it. At 6am I decide to use the autopilot (which I thought didn't work but does). I speak to Angus. He helps a little on the technical side, not on my emotional breakdown (not actually his job). Probably not that massive, but he deserves a 'sorry for being grumpy, tired' text!

The second part of the day results in the autopilot dying (or so I think) or making a noise like it's dying. I can't row and steer so once the autopilot

Day 1

Day 5

Day 10

Day 15

Day 20

Day 25

Day 30

Day 35

Day 40

Day 45

Day 50

needs its rest, I'm told I'll just have to hand steer with the waves. I'll miss my arrival date. I talk to the autopilot and weirdly, it works.

The day brightens and I get some miles in. When night comes, I'm pretty chirpy. Autopilot working, wind in a good direction and a good speed. I get four hours of good uninterrupted sleep and wake up...

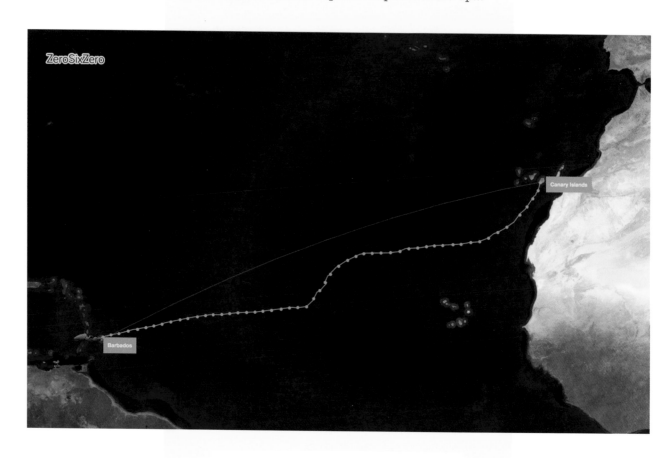

Distance travelled today: 62.60 nautical miles
Total travelled 2,757.34 nautical miles.

# DAY 50

## THURSDAY, 22ND MARCH

I woke up at 5am after an awesome 'mile munching' night and got straight on it. At 9am I jumped into the cabin for a quick snooze only to hear this weird whooshing noise. Peeked outside to find myself marooned in a bed of seaweed the size of three football pitches. It was dark so had no idea which direction to row to escape. Argh – great start to the 'hopefully' last day.

Eventually I was out and the hours passed. Barbados, here I come.

"Angus, I'm nearly there, as long as nothing else goes wrong."

Famous last words. 20 nautical miles from land my GPS dies, then my monitors. The electrics are dying. Yikes. This isn't great, but good old Angus manages to navigate me towards Barbados. The next issue is a potential worry (that I don't do). If the electrics are going down, my autopilot, which I'm sure was on course when the GPS died, goes too. And if that happens I'm going to need to hand steer, which means I won't make it to North Point by dark. I have to make it by dark to meet the pilot boat.

From mile 20 towards Barbados, the boat played ball, the autopilot didn't overheat and Angus's

**Gran Canaria**

Day 1
Day 5
Day 10
Day 15
Day 20
Day 25
Day 30
Day 35
Day 40
Day 45
Day 50

**Barbados**

navigational skills via my tracker were perfect. At 4.30pm Barbados time, I spotted my first human for 49 days; I'd seen my parents flashing me with a mirror, but this was it! The pilot boat, with TV crew and diver on board, would now take me round the island to the point we'd call the finish line.

I talked and talked, telling stories, sharing ideas. Poor guys. It was the camera crew, Sarai and Simon, Anthony the photographer and Brian the man who'd arranged it all.

"Anyone fancy a go?" I offer my boat. No-one wants in. I'm joking of course!

I cannot believe my autopilot made it for the whole night and day – unheard of – they normally die of heat after four to eight hours. It knew this was serious. I cannot believe I was here. I had done 49 days, seven hours and 13 minutes. I could only remember about five of them and I was almost ready to go again.

I saw the lights. This really was it. People cheering. I rowed slowly into the harbour of Port St. Charles, moored up, apologised for being so late and stumbled off.

A relieved Mum and Dad awaited and my brother with an ice cold mojito. My little nephew said it was the best day of his life. So happy and a little bit proud, I suppose. I'd made it, having rowed 2,836 nautical miles in world record time. See, I told you. You can do anything.

Distance travelled today: 61.22 nautical miles
**Total travelled 2,818.56 nautical miles.**

*Photos: Anthony Ball Photography*

# BARBADOS

*Photos: Anthony Ball Photography*

*My family there to welcome me (from left): brother Robin, father Paddy, mum Genevieve and nephew Louis.*

# On Reflection

There I am. Done. Twenty-four hours later, stumbling sideways around the villa in Barbados with nothing more than two seriously dead hands and arms (it's called claw hand). The memories of pain, boredom and frustration gone. The memories of speed, waves, nature, solitude, thinking and freedom left to tell the story. An experience and outcome that will change my life forever. The best bikini body I'd ever had (the only one, actually) and a blank canvas to paint my next chapter on.

Messages flood in and it seems I have done something incredible; something inspiring and something that will change other people's lives. That was the purpose. The record and achievement were great, but this is what touches me and makes me happy. While I write this, I still don't really understand the enormity of what I've done because I have been blessed with the strength to have made it to the end with a smile on my face (95% of the time!).

Life goes on and at time of writing I'm still very much thinking about the next steps. I'm still living in the cabin at the bottom of my friend's garden and I still drive a 14-year-old white van. I haven't changed and doubt I ever will. To be honest, I don't really want to. It's time to move on to the next thing and hopefully inspire more people. The thought of the unknown is exciting. Thinking of all the opportunities, the new people to meet and the new experiences I'll have. I want to lie on my death bed and know that I have been the best me and that I have given back enough to the Earth to thank it for what it gave me. Who knows, I might even find a man, have babies and settle down (but don't hold your breath!).

But what can I give you to take away from my achievement?

It would be great if everyone suddenly realised they were also capable of doing it, although it may prove too great a leap for some. People often comment on my confidence and resilience, and yes, a lot of that came from my upbringing and amazing parents who let me be independent and supported me when things didn't go to plan, but I have also taught myself lots along the way. I'm not a professional rower and had never been to sea so it wasn't as if this was a natural place for me to go. Everything that helped me achieve the record and the fundraising came from my past experience and my behavior. I also never realised what I was creating until very recently and I hope that these realisations may work for you too.

With resilience comes confidence and vice versa. You have to be prepared to fail. It's human nature to challenge ourselves and failure is proof we are doing just that. You have to be willing to accept rejection and understand that it's not always about you. I believe we need to be more aware of ourselves and others and of the environment around us. Stop thinking about 'me' and focus on the 'you' and on nature and what's around us. Don't look for happiness in something material as it won't make you resilient, confident or happy. It's the connections I make, the time spent outdoors, the challenges I have overcome and the experiences I have had that make me happy.

Half way through my training, I came up with Kikonomics. It's a simple concept to help me become more resilient and happier. It's gender irrelevant. In fact, I wish everything was gender irrelevant and we all spent more time focusing on ourselves as a person, not what we should be or how we should behave as men or women. Kikonomics focuses on experiences which help gain resources, and behavior which, if you're getting it right, will give you energy.

When I came up with this concept, everything became clear. I could see how I was energised, confident and happy all the time and how anything felt possible to overcome. When things aren't so great, I actively think about my 'bags'. When they are full, you can tackle anything; when they are low, it's hard and life seems tough. It's up to us as individuals to look after the levels.

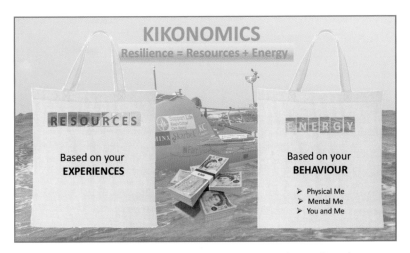

**KIKONOMICS**
Resilience = Resources + Energy

**RESOURCES**

Based on your
**EXPERIENCES**

**ENERGY**

Based on your
**BEHAVIOUR**

➤ Physical Me
➤ Mental Me
➤ You and Me

Resources come from every experience we have. People are resources, skills, understanding, knowledge and physical tools. It is up to the individual to recognize what they can take from these, and the more you do it, the easier it becomes.

Energy comes from three distinct areas. How you behave yourself physically and mentally with others. For me, this is the really important bit. The physical 'me' is what you eat, drink, exercise and sleep. When you are tired or hungover, life is always harder; when you exercise you always feel better afterwards. The mental 'me' is key. This is about passions, honesty, worrying/controlling situations. The honesty part is about knowing who you are and not caring what people think. You'll never please everyone but you want to be around people who like you for who you are, and this goes for your job too. When you understand this, you won't have to waste energy pretending or worrying about who 'you' are. Worrying – I've written about that. So often things are uncontrollable so why let them have a moment in your life. If a 'worry' pops into your head, be aware of what it means, assess the situation and deal with it. Is it controllable?

We need energy and resources to deal with challenges but they also make us happier. Once you create energy in your life, it will self-perpetuate. Things come to you, people want to be part of you; you build a community and that community helps you when you need it. Go fill your bags! Row your own ocean.

*Relaxing on the beach in Barbados shortly after my arrival and (inset) how I looked with Cushing's Disease before my row.*

# ACKNOWLEDGMENTS

The list is endless and I know I'll miss someone out. If I have, please let me know and I'll take you out for a drink as an apology.

100togetHER: Katherine Grainger, Tracey Edwards, Guin Batten. Polly Small, Genevieve Matthews, Joyce Guiness, Alex Corley-Smith, Gini Pappadakis, Emma Stewart, Nicki & Fleur, Maria Roumy, Alex Depledge, Ciara Ferguson, Pinky Lilani and team, Clodagh Muldoon, Jane Galliford, Matthews girls, Victoria Hamblin, Rathbones ladies, Malvern mums, Adelpha, Addie Pinkster & family, Claire Cohen, Habadasher Aske girls, Fabulous Women, Heather Phillips, Sharon Mawby, Alex Mansell, Jane & Charlie Bigham, Ramsden girls, Sue Clarke, Sallee Ponte-Nash, Georgia Thwaites, Claire Glakin, Paula from the gym, Kitty Bhaman (UBS), Louise Whelan (Fit8), Penny Lovell-Sanlam, Santander ladies, Katrina, Emilia and Beatrice Stendrup, Fiona Meredith, Guy & Kristina (Tribe), Julia Stockil, Maeve (THINX), Hereford Cathedral School, Sydenham High School, Malvern St James School, Nicola Fisher, The Priory School, Ella Montgomery, Izzy Camier (PR), Tessa Jennet (PA), Laura Try (Social Media), Ruth Holland, Jonathon Carter, Camilla Klemme, Ciara O'Sullivan, Jess Holliday, Karen Cooper (Website), Elena Sosa Tejerina (Sports psychologist), Mel Paige, Katherine Daire (Fundraising event), Rowan Grace Evans, Emma Watkins (Agora), Antonia Burridge, Angela Sharp (Marketing support), Mollie Pearse, Olivia Wellock (Fundraising manager), Olivia Bolsworth, Phoebe Dugmore (Medical), Michelle Davies, Nyla Sammons (photography), Sarai Carson & Simon Waldock (filming). Peachy Productions (Fundraising event), Zhik (Waterproof clothing), Tribe (Sports nutrition), CurraNZ (Sports supplements), Fortress Marine (Anchor replacement!), Outdoor Food (Freeze dried main meals), Armor-x (Waterproofing and mounts for phones), Gym+Coffee (Athleisure clothing - just love them), Do Sport Live (my shorts I wore day in, day out!), Green People Organic (suntan lotion), Anthony Goddard @ ZeroSixZero (mapping).

All the team at Rannoch Adventure and Charlie for hiring me his boat.

Financial: RW Invest, Aspen Wolfe, Farr Vintners, Skarbeck, Explore What Matters.

Photo: Nyla Sammons